A GOD FOR
A DARK JOURNEY

GENESEE ABBEY LIBRARY
Piffard, New York

A God For A Dark Journey

by

George A. Aschenbrenner, S.J.

BX 2350.2 A8 1984 glas
Aschenbrenner, George A.
A God for a dark journey / by

Computer ID: 48605

Dimension Books • Denville, New Jersey

Published by Dimension Books, Inc.
Denville, New Jersey 07834

ISBN Number - 0-87193-211-3
First American Edition 1984 by Dimension Books

Imprimi potest:
Rev. Joseph P. Whelan, S.J.
Provincial
Maryland Province

Grateful acknowledgement is hereby made to *Review for Religious* for permission to reprint in revised and expanded form Chapters which first appeared in its pages. Copyright © George A. Aschenbrenner, S.J.

All rights reserved. No part of this book may be reproduced in any form without written permission from the publisher, except for brief passages included in a review appearing in a newspaper or magazine.

26089

DEDICATION

For my mother and my father,
for whom the journey is no longer dark.

TABLE OF CONTENTS

INTRODUCTION

Abram became Abraham in a journey of faith. It was a journey that would re-name this ancient man of many years. God's invitation had called him to stand forth and journey far beyond what, at the time of his calling, was familiar and comfortable, what was home to him. The stakes were so high and the risk so awesome that the journey would forge in him a whole new identity. But many obstacles would darken Abram's vision and try his trust before Abraham would be born—born in his own fidelity to God's promise of blessing and fecundity. And born in Abraham there would be a whole new people, as numerous as the stars of the heavens and as the grains of sand on the seashore.

Abraham, as an archetype of faith, has now become a promise and an inspiration for us all. In him we realize that faith is not a thing to clutch in tightly clenched fists. Nor is it a place where we stubbornly stand and settle down. Rather, it is a journey which continually stretches us forward. It is a vision that must daily grow within us. Faith, on this earth, is never complete. And at death it suddenly renders itself useless as it erupts into a white-hot light that unveils One whose intimate love and awesome majesty will, then, defy faith. Abraham's example of freedom and fidelity in the journey of faith stands before us all as a promise of similar blessing and fecundity.

A faith vision gives light to human hearts to find hope and meaning for the journey of daily life in our world. But hope and meaning are neither obvious nor easy before many of the scenes that confront us these days. The early years of this decade have seen almost three hundred members of an international peace-keeping force killed in a terrorist bombing in Beirut. Two hundred and sixty nine people died as a Korean jetliner was shot out of the sky over Russian territory. In El Salvador more than forty thousand people have been killed. Abortions in the United States now surpass an annual one and a half million total—which for many seems to cause no more stir than McDonald's tabulation of hamburgers sold. In Ethiopia and other African nations, and in other parts of our world too, a food crisis continues to starve our brothers and sisters while in the United States food, stockpiled in control of the market, goes to waste. And as the outcry of protest and fear grows more vociferous and extensive, nuclear weapons continue to be built and installed in an insane international bartering for peace. Rather than leading to hope and light and human meaning, our journey together, whatever be the year, often wrestles with despair, darkness and futility. Our journey into the future will require a very special faith vision. A vision so penetrating and compassionate as to find light within the darkness, and thus to maintain hope and enthusiasm as we strive to understand and live God's dream of love and justice in our world.

We need a God for our dark journey. Only a God who could call being out of nothingness and order out of chaos can enlighten the deepest darkness. This God has drawn near to us in Jesus and has become in him a revelation and a promise of faithful presence and love for each of us. The One Jesus called "my dear Father" guided him along the journey of his own life, provided the constant inspiration of love, and radiated light in the darkness of his world. Yes, he was light for Jesus all along the way—and most especially in the chilling loneliness of an olive grove and in the ominous darkness of Calvary. This dear Father quickened the heart of Jesus and became his ALL every step of the way. This Father, this Light, this ALL, was God for him, always inspiring and inviting the next step, even when the step was into the mysterious darkness of his Passion. Finally, this obedient Son's dying was blessed with a fullness of joy and life in Resurrection. And now, Jesus stands for all of us as a revelation and a promise of God's faithful presence and love in every situation of this world. A Son and Father all lost in wonder and union with the endless mystery of one another now send their salvific Spirit to quicken our hearts. And that Spirit is our encouragement and indeed our possibility of always seeking and finding a God of love and light for our dark journey.

This is a book of five annual surveys of the trends and issues in American spirituality. Though these reflections have been stimulated chiefly by my experience in the United States, my travels to other countries have told me that many of the topics treated in this book, with some necessary adaptations, apply beyond American culture and spirituality. As a collection of annual surveys, this book is concerned chiefly with noticing and acknowledging trends and directions in contemporary American spirituality. It is not its intention to provide any significant development

3

of most of the trends it identifies or to provide any resolution for the issues treated. Nor is the book's purpose to divine the future development of American spirituality, though some comments, here and there, do point possible future directions. Rather the book's survey style seeks to highlight a longrange overview of some movements and developments within the ebb and flow of the stream of American spirituality. In this way the book can serve to invite readers to continue their own survey of spiritual trends and issues through further reflection and discussion.

Running through these five surveys is the distinction between a trend and an issue. A trend, here, speaks to a pattern of thought or behaviour, the evidence for which would be sufficiently widespread to make it more than a local or exceptional occurrence. Whereas, as used here, an issue poses alternatives that, unless dodged, invite and eventually even demand a choice. And the choice, of course, often incarnates a whole series of values that relate to and reveal the meaning and understanding of the trend. Often, it is through reflection on a trend that issues are discovered. The more valuable work, I feel, is to look as deeply as possible into current trends in American spirituality, with confidence that this exercise will be of assistance to us in facing the issues which may surface. Many of these issues, it seems to me, do and will continue to need further recognition and clarification before any firm resolution of them is either possible or suitable. Occasionally, however, an issue is so basic, that where one stands on it, where one *should* stand on it, becomes, even early on, clear and fundamental to Christian life. In those cases I have not held back from making a clear judgment about the matter in question.

A certain awkwardness in this book requires comment. The book is made up of five annual articles written in five successive years, from 1980 up to 1984. To have such a one-year gap between each chapter of a book is unusual. But this time gap is built into the very warp and woof of this text. And thus the chapters relate one to another over a quite definite span of time. No effort has been made to conceal this timed aspect of the five annual surveys. Except for minor adaptations to fit the format of this book, the relationship of the articles in their original publication has been left intact.

Finally, it is a joy to give thanks to some people without whom this book could never have happened. My friendship and many discussions with Fr. Joseph Whelan, S.J. clarified and focused much of what I have written. Without the invitation of Fr. Daniel Meenan, S.J., editor of *Review for Religious,* my heart would neither have been sensitized to, nor encouraged to express, my own view of current trends in American spirituality. I am also grateful to the kindly, persistent prodding of Mr. Thomas Coffey, editor of Dimension Books.

Chapter One

LOOKING BACK AT A DECADE: 1970-1980

In a stream there are always different levels of flow. An eddy or a swirl, which does not run so deep as the current, can either spin off and die on the shore or it can get caught up and become part of the deeper current of the stream. It is fascinating and instructive to watch this process.

The last decade has brought an enormous growth in interest and writing about spirituality. This first chapter, focusing on some present issues and concerns of spirituality in this country, will be describing a variety of swirls, eddies, currents and tides within the stream of contemporary spirituality. Generally, this survey does not explicitly distinguish deeper currents from surface motions, but leaves this distinction to the reflection and judgment of the reader. The aim here is simply to list and briefly describe, without any prioritizing, some concerns within contemporary spirituality.[1]

In doing this, I will be consulting both my own experience and the fruits of some conversation with experienced people across the country. At times, I will inject an issue which may not seem of much interest today, but which I personally feel deserves attention. I am aware, of course, that the degree of interest or importance for various concerns will vary according to different geographical sections of the country. But any necessary local nuance is left to the reader.

The survey nature of this chapter, besides severely limiting development of the various concerns expressed, also prevents resolution of them. Sometimes, however, it is the tentative state of the matter itself which allows only an articulation of the question and which requires that any resolution await further clarity in the Spirit. Furthermore, some of the concerns treated in this survey chapter will be developed more in later chapters of this book.

Part I of this chapter presents issues that affect everybody in the Church. Part II treats some matters that touch specific groups: religious, bishops and diocesan priests, lay people.

PART I: ISSUES AFFECTING EVERYONE

1. Distinction between Monastic Apostolic and Active Apostolic Spiritualities. Within the one fundamental Christian spirituality, which, as a following of Jesus, is by definition apostolic, there have always been various spiritualities rooted in different orientations to the one God. Especially since Vatican II, a most helpful clarification has stressed the distinction between monastic apostolic and active apostolic spiritualities. Generally speaking, the monastic experience of God depends upon some physical withdrawal from the world and upon as full an involvement as possible in the liturgy both of the Eucharist and of the Hours, which provides an essential regularity and a rhythm that will determine both the type of community support and the external activity appropriate to this spirituality. Active apostolic experience of God, while deeply located in the activity of the world, requires the difficult combination of an external mobility and dependable spiritual habits, so that one may serve wherever the need for God is greatest. Obviously, this spirituality will provide a different community support, together with both a different presence and a more extensive involvement in the world.

To fail to understand which of the two basic orientations one is called to can cause personal frustration and apostolic ineffectiveness. Disregard of this clarification on the part of the diocesan priest, the religious or the lay person, whether in their training or in the living out of their vocation, may well produce unrealistic expectations and ineffective service. And taking seriously the difference in the two approaches need not imply any superiority of the one over the other. Rather it may help the Church to be more present in the world according to its own fullness and to manifest God's loving designs across the whole spectrum of the human family.

2. *Renewed Monasticism.* After Vatican II there was much questioning and experimentation in reference to the elements of the monastic way of life: enclosure, liturgy of the Hours, community, work, silence, travel, and external apostolic involvement. For a while, the very validity of the monastic life seemed at issue. Now, with its essential validity profoundly reaffirmed, many experiments are being evaluated. This process of evaluation is not concluded but, together with a deep sense that the monastic ideal has been enriched by much of this experimentation, there is a concern as to whether some of the experiments were not motivated by trying too much to

imitate the active life and whether they have not therefore risked weakening the power of the monastic ideal for our age. It will always be a difficult matter to know how, without distorting or superficializing the monastic ideal, its powerful experience of God may be brought into contact with the city.

3. An Integrated, Functional Spirituality for Active Apostles. Excessive fatigue, even to the lengths of burn-out, at times seems almost synonymous with active apostolic work today. Countless demands from so many angles have over-extended and excessively complicated the lives of competent and conscientious men and women. They know the need for formal prayer and a profound, spiritual orientation. And yet there just isn't time for everything. As a result there is not nearly enough formal, personal prayer on the part of many active apostles. And this has serious repercussions, both on the apostles themselves and on all the work they do. And so the search goes on for some functional spirituality that will work for busy apostolic men and women—and work, by giving a sense of integration and unity to their lives.

It is instructive that in the past ten years interest has moved from the topic of discernment of spirits to that of active apostolic spirituality. To my mind, the content is pretty much the same. But the orientation is very different. Discernment of spirits involves chiefly an interpretative sorting out in faith of inner, affective experiences, so that, through dealing properly with the experiences, one can find and be with God in every situation and moment of life. But this process runs the risk of a short-sighted interiority and a spirituality without adequate orientation to apostolic service. Active apostolic spirituality, it would seem, involves the same decisive dealing in faith with inner, affective experiences, but now with a much increased realization that this faith-process within the person gives a special quality of integrated, peaceful presence in the most challenging, active situations—and that this presence, eloquent for God in itself, also leads to actions which further his Kingdom in the world. Dealing in faith with the daily consolations and desolations of life can integrate and unify our whole affectivity and person. And this faith-process certainly does not excuse the active apostle from a program of regular, formal prayer. Rather it reveals the need to discover the unique style of serious, formal prayer appropriate for each individual. Such prayer will always be an essential means to that quality of human presence which reveals a loving Father in Jesus as the Beloved of our hearts and which can find and serve Him in everything.

In this sense, current interest in active apostolic spirituality seems very healthy and very likely to lead both to an apostolic presence that is increasingly prayerful and where activity is therefore not seen as weakening the contemplative presence of prayer, but as a continuation of that contemplative presence beyond the limits of formal prayer. This integrated, apostolic presence will not decrease the demands made on us, but it can prevent the sense of being overly distracted and torn between the dichotomy of formal prayer and apostolic activity. This integrated spirituality can also lessen that sense of dualism against which we are so often warned today.

4. Renouncing the World to Serve It for God. It is not easy for us to see the world from God's perspective and to serve its needs in the light of his dream of justice. Finally, this can be done only by one who comes from an experience of God, an experience in God, back to the world. Though we are usually first led to know and love God, of course, in and through his creation, there must and does come, for those whose experience of God matures, a moment of experiencing him beyond this world's wisdom and potentiality—a moment of experiencing God as not simply equal to, but as far beyond, all the beauty and wisdom of this world. This moment of transcendence, of finding complete satisfaction and joy in a loving God himself, roots our identity primarily in God and gives his love a priority over any created reality. It is an experience that re-announces us before God, before ourselves and before the world as a people of God, a people in God. In this way our "renunciation" (re-announcement) of the world for God puts the world in its true perspective, as seen in and from God.[2] Rather than lessening our interest in the world, this view dramatically increases our zeal to further God's Kingdom in the world and so bring it to its full potential. But serving the needs of our world properly, as part of our love of God, demands this worldly renouncement.

There are issues of some importance for active apostles today that relate to this renunciation of the world. Can this experience of renunciation happen without some physical withdrawal from the world? And since the renunciation referred to here is not a once-in-a-lifetime experience, what means will help active people to keep it alive and growing as a per-

11

sonal attitude? With much less physical detachment from the world in most seminaries and novitiates (and much of this is good and in accord with the appropriately non-monastic training of active apostles), how can we be assured that this necessary attitude of renunciation is taking permanent root in the apostle's consciousness? How do active apostles prevent this worldly renunciation either from turning into a withdrawal from the world which, while suitable for monks, is most unsuitable for them, or, even worse, from turning into an unChristian lack of concern for the world? The American Church is not finished with these questions. We need more discussion, and better answers. For without this attitude of worldly renunciation, we may have active apostles busy doing many good things, but not perceiving the world's full potential for beauty and goodness and not furthering the reality of a Father's Kingdom that is revealed chiefly in a dead Son's Resurrection.

5. Relationship of Spirituality and Morality. For too many people morality has been corrupted by an overly narrow, moralistic and rationalistic stress. This moralism, with its rationalistically detailed stress on casuistry, tends to cut healthy morality off from its roots in the spirituality of God's revelation. It has caused much unhealthy fear, guilt and introspection. The holy person was proposed as one who avoided a clearly delineated list of mortal and venial sins. And too often, this avoidance of sins seemed more a matter of stubbornly pelagian will power than a matter of prayerfully humble dependence on God's grace.

But now, conversely, it seems one could be taking means for serious growth in prayer, faith and a spiritual life, and yet this spiritual seriousness need not express itself in quite practical matters like the morality of public, social affairs or of a chaste sexual life. At times, neither certain social injustices nor something like masturbation is seen as unholy and thereby affecting one's love relationship with God. The intertwined strands of spirituality and morality are here become so unraveled that holy, prayerful Christian people may not be expected to come to similar moral conclusions on various practical issues.

A fuller view of both morality and spirituality, however, rather finds them mutually inclusive and affirming of one another, mutually accountable, while at the same time leaving to each its own, appropriately specific, stress. To view some practical matter spiritually is to judge its appropriateness against the faith-ideal of a trust in God's loving power wonderfully filling our own weakness whenever it is exposed in self-emptying surrender. In this way certain attitudes, dispositions and actions are unholy and unspiritual because they violate this trust in God's love. Only one's spiritual growth in union with God will provide this trust in the practical details of daily living.

Much is being done these days in moral theology to resurrect a modern version of full, healthy Christian morality and spirituality as integral to each other. A very interesting issue in this new approach in moral theology is the role in moral decision making which prayerful discernment of spirits plays in providing that moral knowledge whereby a holy person can know God's love in a concrete situation.

6. Sin—Forgiveness—Sacrament of Reconciliation. Related to the previous consideration of spirituality and morality is another issue: our personal experience as sinners in the human reception of God's vivifying forgiveness in and through the sacrament of reconciliation. Although there are unhealthy dualisms which deny integral human living and which should therefore be avoided, the dualism of a person saved in Jesus but with much affective evidence of sinfulness cannot be avoided. This dualism is the very setting for the Christian adventure of sons and daughters still gradually coming into their own. The seven capital sins, alive in our affective consciousness as dispositions, inclinations and impulses, provide us with our own version of the pauline divided heart.[3] But we have an indestructible hope of ever more healing and wholeness in the crucified Son's discovery of his Father's blessing of resurrection.

Continual conversion, so central to the Christian life, happens in the painfully, purifying humiliation of a double acknowledgement: my personal sinfulness, and the faithful love of the Trinity for me in the Son's Calvary experience. And this brings in turn a double awareness: we are never nearly so good as we try to make ourselves out to be; but we are far more loved in the Trinity's forgiveness than we could ever imagine. This process of personal assimilation of God's forgiveness is neither instantaneous nor superficial. The inner humiliation of an unqualified admission of personal sinfulness before our beloved Father in his crucified Son is something that we instinctively shy away from. In this experience, a careful discernment of what is spiritually good for each person is needed.[4]

Despite the reform of the rite of the sacrament of reconciliation, I wonder whether people are being helped to deepen their experience of this growth to self identity through forgiveness. The old superstructure surrounding the institution of frequent confession has broken down—as it had to. Reconciliation prayer services have restored the communal dimension of sinfulness and forgiveness within the community of the Church, and a whole new format has been developed for the individual reception of the sacrament of reconciliation. But there are ways in which a communal experience of the sacrament, without a carefully personal and individual experience, can superficialize or short-circuit the human process of receiving God's forgiveness. As we grow to a more healthy and loving sense of ourselves, we can learn to find the individual experience of the sacrament a helpful means of growth to the maturity of humble trust in the fidelity of the Trinity's forgiving love always available in our weakness.

7. Faith and Justice. After the topic of prayer, this seems the theme most treated in today's spiritual writing. Many persons are much more sensitive today to the systemic network of social sin that is rooted in the individual sinfulness of human hearts—hearts radically social in nature. But we have a long way to go in developing a sensitivity for social sin and a social morality. And the insight that justice in a sense much fuller than simply its social-political meaning, is integral to faith badly needs to grow in the Church. Opportunities for such growth are being very well served by current studies in scripture[5] and in Christology.[6]

Further study and reflection, however, is needed to recognize more precisely the sense of justice that is so centrally related to Christian faith—the full paschal justice of God, motivated and revealed in us through a refined and decisive faith. It is the zealous faith of a great love of God that urges on us passionate concern and practical involvement for the justice of God's Kingdom. For we are not urged on *simply* by a social theory about the unity of the human family, or about communal ownership of our earth's resources, or about the inherent evil of war. The fundamental and difficult question of how Christianity relates to various political ideologies—and to ideology as such—arises here. In South America the question of the possibility of a Christian marxism is very alive, whereas in this country there is a serious questioning of the assumptions of capitalism. These are complicated questions about specific situations and activities. But we must remember that zeal for the justice of God's Kingdom can never be limited simply to the matter of a specific kind of activity that one is involved in. Rather, and with more far ranging, quite practical effect, it must grow to a vision that pervades and influences everything we do.

A few other aspects of this issue deserve listing. The tendency to an excessively introspective, privatized spirituality needs the challenge of that zeal for justice which validates a person's faith.[7] We must learn how to relate our zeal for justice to our contemplation. For active apostles in the heat of unjust, oppressive situations, it is never easy to believe in the grace to convert understandable angry feelings into the appropriate expression of tenderness and compassion. Much more than a matter of a given temperament, we must see tenderness and compassion not as unbecoming to either a man or a woman in certain situations, but as virtues contemplatively rooted by grace in a person's affectivity and will. Finally, many of us need new experiences to help us feel much more passionately the tangled questions this issue raises, before we can even know the question, much less the answers.

8. Role of Women in the World and the Church. Another major concern in spirituality today is the role of women. The issue, understandably enough, is often so fraught with crusading passion and angry feelings that, as a man who surely does not feel enough the seriousness of the issue, one almost fears to say anything at all.

Against a backdrop of past and present prejudice, the leadership role of women in the Church slowly increases. But there is a long way to go. Attitude, rather more than language, seems nearer the heart of the matter—and yet linguistic care both expresses and shapes our attitude. And the attitude of many leaders and other people in the Church must profoundly change before women will exercise a suitably influential role and make their unique contribution (something any exaggerated uniformity and equality, of course, will not allow).

In general, there seem to be three stages to this concern. First is an awareness of the fact of past injustice, however it is explained. This is often followed by a period of intense reaction, which is quite understandable, whether apparently exaggerated or not. Finally, a stage of peaceful service in the Church is often reached, as one does what is possible to correct the injustice. It is a process similar to Kubler-Ross's stages[8] and has been gone through by others when facing the deadly situation of unjust discrimination.

Women's ordination to the priesthood is of course still debated. For many, however, it does not seem to be the heart of the issue at the present time. Much will continue to be accomplished without changing the present policy on women's ordination to the ministerial priesthood. This does not deny that there are painful situations, which can be paschally productive for all, in which women actually minister a "sacramentally" salvific experience without the acknowledged ministerial priestly capacity formally to celebrate the experience in the Church. A good example of this is the woman director of a retreat who cannot administer the sacrament of reconciliation after sharing a retreatant's graced experience of God's forgiveness. Many would feel—and many would not—that this is still an open question, about which the Church seems not to have enough light in the Spirit to know whether a change is called for or not.

In the meantime, we all need to grow in a sensitivity to correct past injustice in our own relationships, to beg for light in the Spirit regarding what is the right growth in this issue for the future, and to pray for the humility and the urgent patience of Jesus in his passion to live and serve generously in the present situation.

9. *Spirituality and Psychology.* Because spirituality involves the total human person in relationship to God's saving love, it can be related to every area of human behavior. It is especially appropriate and valuable to relate spirituality to psychology, and over the past decade or more interest in this relationship has increased enormously. As an

overly rationalistic view of spirituality subsides, we investigate much more the role of the non-rational dimensions of our person in spiritual growth. Spirituality can be naive, and destructive too, when it flies in the face of healthy psychology. But spirituality loses its salvific power for the human person, and becomes equally demonic, when it capitulates completely to psychology. A delicate balance is called for in this relationship—something not easily arrived at, or easily preserved.

In turning to some specific aspects of this general issue, it is obvious that much greater stress is now being placed on communication skills, on affectivity, on the role of the body, and on consciousness-altering techniques—all of which can enrich our prayer and further sensitize us to the many ways God's word and love come to us. The practice of spiritual direction often legitimately overlaps with a type of psychological counseling. But the ultimate aim of facilitating union with God must always clearly distinguish spiritual direction from professional counseling. If it is true that the most pervasive heresy in the Church today is the lack of healthy self-acceptance and self-love, then some basic remedial work on the self-concept is an essential task of spiritual direction for most people. This psychological dimension, if not carefully handled and integrated with spirituality, can run the risk of a narcissistic infatuation with the self.

Serious dialogue between professionals in spirituality and psychology will further the relationship. But perhaps the person with a rich and holy faith life who also seriously trains in psychology will make the best contribution.

10. Fidelity and Perseverance. We live in a post "future shock" culture. In 1970 Alvin Toffler wrote *Future Shock,* and chapter one was entitled: The Death of Permanence.[9] He said we would be shocked because our future culture would be characterized by transience, disposability, novelty and mobility. The very air we breathe is now charged with these qualities. In some ways the qualities of this "future shock" are exactly the opposite of permanence, perseverance and fidelity. And yet, we cannot just stop the world and get off. Statistics about the divorce rate, priests' and religious' leaving their commitments, the closing of Catholic schools, and the stopping of various inner-city apostolates can scare us. But the judgment of infidelity in any single instance of these examples is not easily made. Speaking in general, however: Is the matter of persevering with a commitment previously made, come what may, still a spiritual ideal? Surely it is not the cultural ideal today. Such currents in our culture clearly challenge our spirituality. And they can enrich it too—they can enhance our freedom and our service—if we are not simply swept along by their tidal force, but are carefully discerning in our evaluation and adaptation.

In discussing the matter of fidelity and various commitments, I do not intend to imply any personal culpability of infidelity on another's part. Each individual's case is so unique and intricate that a human judgment is almost impossible. A recent good phenomenon in the Church has been the appearance of groups for service (sometimes partially or wholly made up of former religious) in which members are not bound together by fidelity to a permanent commitment. At the same time, in groups identified by the bond of permanent commitment, we must learn how to live that particular, quite specific faith experience which is God's fidelity promised to a person in the covenant of a permanent choice. Further understanding is required concerning the way in which, for a particular individual, fidelity to the baptismal covenant can be expressed in, and even identified with, the permanent commitment of marriage, priesthood, religious life. At times it may be too easily argued that one leaves one of the latter to preserve fidelity to the former, the baptismal covenant. To move to the future from a fundamental life-option which has been chosen, does close off other fundamental life-options. But persevering with the chosen option can often bring a greater awareness of one's own inner resources, a deepening of trust in God, and the joyous surprise of his faithful presence in everything.

There is much mystery in all of this. And it is important not to give the impression that public expressions of Christian fidelity and perseverance are, in every case, simple and clear. But the matter is of immense import. For Christian fidelity and perseverance, though it is surely counter-cultural in this country, allows the Church to provide some stability and continuity amidst the rushing waters of discontinuity in our culture. This continuity in and through the prevailing discontinuity is something many people are looking for, and it just may be critical to the survival of the humanity of this nation's culture.

11. Eastern Influences. The turning to the East for spiritual enrichment continues in western Christianity. While raising some questions for further investigation, this eastern influence has affected western Christians in various ways. Some few have abandoned Christianity for eastern approaches and methods. Others are trying to synthesize the mystical spirituality of the East with the more rational ways of the West. Still others have been stimulated by contact with the East to search for the often-overlooked mystical element in our western tradition.[10]

There has been much written about the destructive force for contemplation and wonder that western technology is. There is truth to this—enough that some may feel one must become a cultural drop-out in order to learn to pray and to be contemplatively open to God's loving presence. But a more subtle, valuable question concerns how to manage, in both theory and practice, ways in which technology can promote true American, Christian spirituality. To develop a spirituality which can guide and orient the development of technology is far more difficult—and, I would think, far more valuable than either to write off the whole of technology, or to be helplessly swept along by the technological tide.

Eastern prayer approaches are much in use. As this influence on our practice of prayer develops, some difficult issues arise. Can eastern prayer methods that were originally non-Christian and which may even have developed in a tradition in which grace does not exist be validly used by a Christian? For one who believes that God is at the center of the self and of all reality, can't the quiet sitting of Zen or a centering exercise be an experience of God, and not just a restful and humanly renewing experience? What "proof" do we have inside or outside the consciousness of the one praying to answer this question one way or the other? As we continue to investigate experientially these questions, hopefully the meeting of East and West will provide mutual spiritual enrichment.

12. Leisure and Contemplation. One thing most active apostles have very little of is leisure. Because of some eastern influence, there is more concern now with the necessary role of leisure in avoiding the commercialization of our humanity, and in facilitating a dimension of contemplative wonder to our person and presence. The phenomenon of burn-out among apostles and the confrontation with technology's dehumanizing possibilities have also raised this concern.

It is important to see leisure not simply as time set apart like a vacation, but as a dimension of how we live and work each day.[11] Leisure cannot be another ingredient to add to the already complicated mixture of a busy day. If it can be integrated as part of our approach to daily life, then it can make the difference spiritually between the pelagian busy strivings of the workahaolic and the peaceful, graceful presence of the apostle whom God uses to further his Kingdom in many human hearts and structures.

13. The Charismatic Movement. A major spiritual influence in the Church in recent years has been the charismatic movement. While revitalizing the dead or complacent faith of many people, it has stirred an enormous interest in prayer.

The early graced enthusiasm of prayer and faith must mature and deepen. Members of the movement especially need to be helped to grow beyond an early, superficial stage in the pilgrimage of prayer. The powerfully moving communal prayer of meetings must be rooted in the regular practice (not always so moving!) of formal, individual prayer and in daily lives of service in society. As the Christian life continues to mature, there occurs a refinement of the ability to discern the presence of the Holy Spirit, guided by rational ecclesial norms and those perceptible signs of the Spirit's presence in human situations.[12] This discernment in the members, beyond the Life in the Spirit Seminar, is an important, needed development in the movement. In the early enthusiastic stages of conversion and faith-growth, fundamentalism is often a danger and it seems to manifest itself at times in various groups of the movement. This fundamentalistic spirit is always divisive, at least eventually, and can cause some problem with the movement's deeper integration into the Church. Real advance has been made, it seems, in dealing with this issue. And now some members are concerned with the relation of charismatic authority and church office—a more subtle aspect of the movement's fitting into the Catholic Church and its witness in the world today.[13]

The movement's achievements are notable. The areas for further growth that have been singled out would not be possible except that the movement is so firmly settled in the Church and in the lives of many believers. It has brought to spirituality a renewed sense both of the communal sharing of faith life and of the joy and enthusiasm (more than sheer emotion) that should characterize one who lives in God's love.

14. Mutual Trust Allowing Cooperation, Delegation and Subsidiarity of Responsibility. Because the challenge and work facing the Church today far exceed the competence and energy of any one individual or group, there is a much greater need for cooperation in all apostolic effort. This cooperation must learn to reach across borders not commonly crossed in days gone by. One of the many possible examples is the parish where pastor, curate, religious and lay persons must all cooperate. The search continues for the appropriate forms of this cooperation. But right at the core of the issue is humility and forgiveness, as the conditions for a cooperative attitude on the part of all. Without mutual trust, which often today cannot be presumed, there will be little such cooperation and even less delegation of real responsibility in true subsidiarity. And without this mutual trust and cooperation, the growth of God's Kingdom in our complex world is positively interfered with.

PART II: ISSUES AFFECTING SPECIFIC GROUPS

The issues described in Part I affect all groups in the Church in this country in some way or other. However, for some specific groups, either there are specialized applications of general issues or there are new issues in spirituality that have not yet been mentioned. Part II, then, will describe some few issues specific to religious, bishops and diocesan priests, and lay people.

A. Religious

1. Obedience, Unity, and Submission to Religious Authority. Obedience is rarely talked of in some religious congregations, which makes for wonder as to whether it is practiced anymore, while in other groups it is much discussed in relation to religious authority and individual responsibility. In the past ten years, obedience has developed a lot in relationship both to mission and to the unity of congregations. However, I do not think the specific implications of this healthy development have always been seen.

The obedience of "being sent" to participate in Jesus' mission from his Father is an attitude of heart in each member that can bring a deep unity among all. "Being sent" and "sending oneself" are fundamental alternatives, though perhaps not always easily distinguished in the individual's interior attitude and the involvement with the religious superior[14] in the process of apostolic assignment. Though the individual has a maturely responsible role to play in this assignment, the final decision rests with the superior. The attitude of "being sent" finally takes effect in a moment of utter receptivity before God—a receptivity expressed in the individual's submission to the religious authority of another human person who is the superior. As understood today, this act of submission is not an infantile cop-out in the face of parental authoritarianism. Rather it is an incarnational obedience, a quite personal, adult finding of Christ our Lord that is mediated within the Church and which brings a spiritual joy and freedom and zeal to serve. In a governmental structure for apostolic assignments where this fully adult submission is not possible, I doubt that true religious obedience is possible, and I doubt that, in the long run, apostolic service is really enhanced. It seems time for the period of under-

standable reaction to past authoritarian excess to be
declared over and for full play to be given to the
graced call to the mature, spiritual demands of the
full process of religious, incarnational, apostolic obedience.[15]

2. *Appropriate Expressions of Affection in
Celibate Friendship.* There is not much concern now
with the profound spiritual and theological meaning
of religious celibacy in the Church. This does not in-
dicate a lack of belief in this meaning. Johannes Metz
has raised the political or practical element of celibacy
(and of all the vows).[16] But I feel there is another
aspect of celibacy that is of even more concern today,
though it is not often talked of or written about in
public: the appropriate expression of affection in intimate, celibate love relationships.

The number of intimate friendships in which at
least one of the parties is celibate, continues to increase. This friendship is always a precious gift from
God, not only to the persons involved but to the
whole Church. In a period of puritanical sexual
repression this gift is not truly appreciated. When
given, it is God's gift, and the ones involved must
always stay free to receive the gift in each daily situation, rather than grasp it and control it for the
future—a move which will surely destroy its apostolic
beauty and effectiveness.

Intimate friendship must always be expressed if it
is to be lived and treasured. To find the proper expression of the special affection growing between two
people is not always easy, and yet it is rarely talked
about. What are the expressions of affection that
violate celibacy? How will the persons involved

know? Let me use one example to show how complex this issue can be. Is there an experience between a man and a woman of holding and being held which is an end in itself? If so, it is not simply a means of expression in a special situation, as after a long separation or at a time of great grief. Rather it is an expression, good and beautiful, and valid in itself, of the commitment and love that marriage validates between a man and a woman. Though this special experience of "being held" is attractive to everyone, might it be an expression of affection that violates celibate commitment? I am asking questions here. I do not at all intend to imply an inhuman fear of touching and being touched, so essential for full humanity and quite different from the experience of being held I am referring to. Issues such as this are important as we grow in living the celibate commitment. Mistakes can be made by sincere, generous people, who just don't know or who are swept beyond the limits of control by passion—that powerful and beautiful human force in each of us. For this reason we cannot always trust ourselves in these situations. And yet where does one go for help?

Related to the specific question of affective expression of celibate friendships is the matter of what used to be called "the third way," which is not so publicly discussed anymore—though I am not sure it is less frequent. While appreciating the great human enrichment of more healthy, heterosexual celibate relationships, I wonder whether there is clarity enough about sexual and affective signs of a dating relationship. I wonder whether in religious life, without any formal intention, there can grow that immature adolescent phenomenon of a "singles mentality." These sexual, affective aspects of the celibate life are a concern today, especially in the midst of a culture where sexual mores and morality are in great revolution.[17]

3. Religious Poverty and Simplicity. In recent years the countless hours spent in discussion of poverty among religious have often produced more heat and fury than real light. Yet religious communities need as much light as they can have about how poverty and simplicity relate to the total charism of the group, for this light must guide the discernment of the practice of poverty within the group.

For some groups poverty is meant to be simplicity. For others it is much more than simplicity. In a world which talks of trying to resolve massive economic and sociological poverty, it is important to distinguish the spiritual motivation for religious poverty. The lack of enough affectively intimate experience of our Father's love for us in his crucified Jesus is one reason why we often are not poor enough. If our true identity is not rooted in our Father's satisfying love for us in his crucified Son, then we are not capable yet of the ideal of religious poverty whereby, in a very counter-cultural way, our identity is not rooted in material possessions. The interplay between religious and economic poverty and between poverty of spirit and actual poverty is never easy, but striving for the right synthesis of these elements can be very creative for individuals.[18]

A second reason, never sufficiently motivating in its own right, why we often are not poor enough is the lack of experience of actual contact with the sociological poverty of our world. Without exploiting poor people, various programs try to provide experiences which can focus an immediate apostolic dimension and need for religious poverty. Granting the varieties of practice of poverty according to the charisms of different groups, we must sometimes get to the practical level, where poverty does mean less possessions and spending less money as a sign against our American consumer society. This can be a very practical step that anyone can work on. And yet, the heart of the matter runs much deeper than things, to an attitude of free surrender of the total self to a God whose love in Jesus suffices. In this way religious poverty is closely related to the surrender of self involved in obedience and in celibate chastity.[19]

One final aspect would be the need to rediscover an appropriate contemporary *communal* mode of poverty—in which poverty would bind the members of a community together in an intimate, joyous unity. This would require poverty to be much more than just an individual—or even a communal—matter of budget and frugality. To grow and survive it would have to be the bond of love it was for the founding members of many congregations.

4. Community Support in New Forms. In many places, the uniform mode of large communities has broken down into many different shapes and forms. But the issue of needed community support to live celibacy and apostolic commitment joyously is not resolved. Religious life ought to provide a great deal of solitude. But it ought not be unduly lonely. If it is, then marriage will, indeed should, seem more attractive. We would expect the many other changes in religious life since Vatican II to have repercussions on the quality of felt support and sharing in community life. Men and women who are doing satisfying and valuable apostolic work can still be dissatisfied because of what they consider to be a lack of community support and sharing. I suggest the most critical failure often is the lack of appropriate ways to share our spiritual faith-ideal, whether in prayer or in other ways. Without some implicit and some quite explicit sharing of our faith identity, we become, depending on the size of the community, either fellow apartment dwellers or residents of the same hotel. This impoverishes the apostolic person. And it thereby impoverishes apostolic choice and action as well.

Together with some sharing of our identity in faith, we must also, as indicated, allow the physical and psychological space for the solitude which is at the core of each person's celibate commitment.[20] This can be a difficulty in small communities. When this type of celibate solitude is overlooked, the individual can unknowingly be looking for the community to be a marital companion—something it can never provide. Even though the community be comprised of people involved in various works, we must also find a way to tie this sharing of faith identity and personal solitude into the mission orientation of the community. So many times mission orientation is an individual matter and is neither felt nor expressed communally. And the plethora of new forms of religious community should not defeat us. If we remain clear on the essential elements of shared faith-identity, celibate solitude, and mission orientation, and if we experiment with ways of expressing these elements together,

31

we can find the different ways for different communities to grow together and support all the
members. No doubt, some new and old community
forms will die along the way.

Though the polarity between two fundamentally
different views of religious life (not always split according to old and young) is perhaps less public and
less intensely expressed than it used to be, it has not
been completely resolved. It simmers underneath talk
of unity. It may be that this will gradually be resolved
by serving together the world's real needs. But I
wonder if we won't need to reveal somehow to one
another that evidence of fundamental unity which
would disprove what many claim has actually happened: that some of our congregations have actually
split into two quite different versions of originally
unified groups.

5. *Sense of Church and How To Fit In*. More
and more religious feel an alienation from the institutional Church, whether it be because of
misunderstandings and differences of opinion with
the hierarchy and clergy or with the general run of lay
people. A distance is created which can lead the
religious' spirituality to become a private matter,
quite alienated from the Church. A habit of informal,
spontaneous liturgies often makes the ordinary parish
liturgy seem almost intolerable. And through such
behavior, whatever it may be, attitudes form, attitudes often never articulated by the individual but
which are very real and influential. Blame in this complicated situation is not easy to assign. But rather
than being allowed to go underground, the problem
needs recognition, and it needs dialogue that is
marked by great patience.

The relationship of religious life to the Church as a whole is described by Metz in his book on religious life: "a kind of shock therapy instituted by the Holy Spirit."[21] We should not therefore expect the relationship always to be simple, easy and tranquil. But it is important that religious are men and women of the Church, with a deep belief in and love of the institutional-charismatic Church. It is possible for religious, whether because they are too progressive or too reactionary, to be working in their own small area and ministry, quite oblivious of the whole Church's ministry and the international stage of our world.

But together with these difficulties related to a sense of the Church, there is also among the religious a deep ecclesial sense, and this brings with it a recognition of the plurality of ministries in the Church and a desire to serve and be part of the Church in her world-wide ministry of God's peace, love and justice. In fact, this growth in appreciation and love of the Church is what causes anguish and pain for those who meet much misunderstanding and difference of opinion in a specific parish, or on other levels of Church membership.

6. *How Institutions Today Further God's Kingdom.* The institutional involvement of many religious groups is very heavy. Often this has become a big financial burden, which determines much of the apostolic orientation of the group and does not allow much serious questioning of the involvement itself. And frequently enough, there are fewer and fewer members available and eager to work in such institutions. At the same time, there is such a stress today on direct and immediate service of the world's social

33

needs that a real prejudice against the institutional approach often builds up. It is an attitude that can influence new members quickly. The right approach to this problem is not always obvious. But what is essential on the part of each member is the spiritual freedom to confront the situation honestly, with a readiness either to withdraw or to move more deeply into a particular institution, reorienting it to serve long-range changes in society, for the furthering of God's Kingdom.

7. *The Freedom to Die.* I cannot really imagine the effect on a congregation of receiving no new members for five or more consecutive years, and of watching the total number of members gradually drop below one hundred. Only the members of such a group can really know this experience. And even for them it is often hard to face the implications and to try to read God's word in the event. I know secondhand that this situation can provoke great spiritual challenge and individual renewal. In his book, Metz talks of "the charismatic art of dying" of religious congregations today.[22] For some groups, the signs seem to be calling for the spirituality to face honestly the prospect of the group's dying. This, of course, is a very painful experience that reveals difficult unfreedoms in various members. But it can also win from God's ever faithful love and care the precious and profound freedom that either can allow a group to die or that can accept a new life and growth for the same group, from its dying embers. This is a freedom we would all like to have. But it is often given only in situations of radical life or death.

B. Bishops and Diocesan Priests

1. Bishops—Prayerfully Pastoral Leaders. The busy pace and enormous responsibility of a bishop are hard for us to appreciate. The tremendous problems with finances and personnel in most dioceses continue to increase. In this situation there are great pressures crowding a bishop into the roles of business manager and administrator. Certain skills in this area obviously are necessary. But whenever this job description as a business manager becomes the primary view of a bishop's role, something has gone profoundly wrong.

It is not easy, however, to fight off the pressures to be primarily a business manger. What means can be provided to help these men be prayerfully sensitive pastors providing real enlightened, spiritual leadership? Some experience of retreats (even of 30 days) for bishops should be continued. Some communal support, whether with other bishops or with the persons the bishop lives and works with, and the possibility of spiritual direction, may provide an opportunity to share personal faith life and to continue the inspiration of retreat experiences. In the long run, it is hard to think of a more important project both for bishops to schedule into their crowded calendar and for retreat directors to provide.

It is also essential that a bishop and his staff welcome and even seek out the cooperation of priests, religious and lay people in running the whole ministry of the diocese. This simply has to involve a real sharing of responsibility leading to structural realignments within the diocese and new relationships of the bishop with various diocesan groups. In 1978, directives for the mutual relations between bishops and religious in the Church were promulgated by the Congregation for Bishops and the Congregation for Religious. These directives spell out just one of these relationships.[23]

    2. Priests—Prayerful Spiritual Directors for the People. Some of what has been said about a bishop's situation can be repeated here. The good popular priest, in touch with the people, is often a very over-worked and fatigued person. He is on the go from morning till late at night trying to respond to the countless demands being made of him. It is easy for prayer to be limited to daily Eucharist and a speedy version of the liturgy of the hours—when there is time or wakeful consciousness even for that. But the qualities of peace, humble confidence, trust and zeal to serve, which belong at the core of a priest's being and action are not possible without regular, personal contemplation alone with God. Such regular prayer transforms the person and thereby gradually transforms the busy day and makes possible a greater sense of God's presence in all.

    Priests must first realize the problem of regular prayer in busy lives, and then seek help. Help can be given in retreats and in other experiences that provide spiritual direction and growth in prayer. Furthermore, in this way, and without very much additional special or professional training, diocesan priests can provide a dimension of spiritual direction to their parish. Some of this will be in individual sessions with parishioners. But it can also be accomplished in homilies of a certain kind, in the sacrament of reconciliation, in other parish activities, and through the general image and presence that the priest has in the parish.

In too many cases, this image and presence of spiritual director is not true of the parish priest, and this is discouraging for religious and lay people who are looking for it. However, to re-image the parish priest in a way that allows him the role of spiritual director may also involve a redistribution of responsibilities in the work of the parish and a certain understanding of the priesthood. This takes us to our next issue.

3. Collaboration in Running the Parish. In many parishes, as competent and well-trained lay people and religious get more involved in the work of the parish, priests can feel threatened, inferior and inadequate. And it is impossible to hide this, even if it is masked over by a firm, almost angry refusal of help in running the parish. A certain frustrating ambivalence may be added to this angry sense of inferiority, when the priest realizes that he cannot keep running the whole parish all by himself. This is very directly related to the fourteenth general concern in Part I. A lot of the disaffection of lay people and religious for the Church comes from their sensing that their competence and desire to help either is not accepted or is relegated to a low level of participation where no real responsibility for the parish is shared. They get the impression that the priest is still in total charge and they are second-class members.

These ambivalent, inferior feelings on the part of the priest must be dealt with before a real fundamental trust can grow which will allow cooperation in the running of the parish. And while we are still in the midst of badly needed changes in the Church with reference to the roles of women, lay people and religious, there will continue to be confusion and hurt feelings about the organization of authority and responsibility in the parish and about the image and role of the priest. We must realize this situation is serious. It determines many people's involvement with, or alienation from, the Church. We are all called to reach out in mutual trust, forgiveness and dialogue, believing in the guidance of the Holy Spirit.

4. *Meaning and Image of the Priesthood.* This is a profound issue affecting the spirituality of the priest. Growth in appreciation of the priesthood of the faithful has brought an increased desire to serve and be involved on the part of many lay people. It has naturally clouded the formerly clear image of ministerial priesthood, and this has had some serious effects on many priests. Is priesthood simply a series of actions, whether done regularly or only every once in a while? Is the ambit of that work much narrower now, and may many priests look forward to being almost completely "out of work" some day? Is the priesthood superior to the lay life, or not? Many priests have strong feelings about these questions. They even have prejudiced answers in some cases. These are important matters, whether directly faced or subconsciously felt, and they have a consequently deep effect on a priest's peace and spirituality.

It will take time to see how the contemporary Church will continue to understand the ministerial priesthood as an identity of being as well as a functional role, even as it recovers the gospel center of ministerial priesthood as a serving within the priesthood of all the faithful—an insight that urges all priests to serve as brother in cooperation with other brothers and sisters in the whole people's growing in that Spirit of Jesus which unites all in praising: Abba, dear Father.

C. Lay People (I use the term "lay," though in many ways it has taken on a pejorative connotation after the days of Catholic Action and so much clericalism. Though canonically the term may make a clear distinction, we need a new term to refer to those people who are not priests or religious, but who are called by God to be the massive body and strength of the Church in its mission to the world.)

1. Growth in Prayer and Spirituality. There is an increasing number of lay people today with real theological training and spiritual experience. The dangerous phenomenon of a lay person maturely trained in some secular profession but with a childishly immature quality of faith and religious experience is still too extensive, but it is steadily decreasing. This is an encouraging sign and an essential part of the Church's renewal. Let me not be misunderstood. In terms of overall numbers, there is an immensely long way to go. But we are not where we were ten years ago.

The need remains, nevertheless, to provide means to help lay people mature in their practice of prayer and their whole life of faith. This never happens automatically—without inspiration, encouragement and some direction. As this spiritual growth occurs among the laity, there is need for supervisory training of lay people to be spiritual facilitators and directors for many others. Training future directors can have an important multiplier effect in the face of growing needs. Though spiritual centers and retreat houses, when they have well-trained personnel, can provide special services, the chief resource center for this ordinary spiritual growth among lay people should be the parish. But this is often not the case.

2. *Parish—Often Not a Center for Spiritual Growth.* As mentioned before, the experience of many competently trained and maturely spiritual lay people leads to disaffection with their parish. They do not find a concentration on contemporary spiritual growth in liturgies, homilies, opportunities for special groups, requests for responsible lay cooperation in parish work, and in the whole spirit of the parish. This is a very discouraging experience. Often, to blame the priest is far too simple, because the priest's training did not give operative priority to spiritual things and so did not ready him to provide any real spiritual orientation to parish life. Well prepared lay people are themselves often better equipped to provide this spiritual orientation. But this of course produces that sense of inferiority and inadequacy in the priest which I discussed earlier.

In all dioceses now there is a large number of former religious and resigned priests. These people constitute a very special group in a parish or diocese. They usually have had more than an ordinary spiritual training. Once they have worked through their feelings about leaving, many of them enter into parish life with a great desire for help and inspiration in continuing their spiritual life—often in the completely different setting of married life. These competently trained men and women frequently have jobs that can be apostolically very influential with large groups of people. So it is a group with great potential for furthering God's Kingdom. What Church leader in a diocese is compassionately concerned about them and in touch with them? How are they helped in the profound reorientation of their lives and in continuing their spiritual growth and service in the Church?

To have the parish serve much better the spiritual growth of the ordinary lay person and of such a special group as former religious and resigned priests will take a lot of work. The rare phenmenon of a seminary's giving clear and decisive priority (a novitiate?) to spiritual things during a definite period of the training of priests must grow and spread much more. For as priests bring an informed and experienced spiritual orientation to their work, the atmosphere of the whole parish will be more conducive to the cooperation and spiritual growth of everyone.

3. A Lay Spirituality of Public Service. As lay people grow in their own spiritual lives and avoid the religious-secular split so pervasive in today's world, and as they intentionally join the Church's ministry of service, we must continue to develop a lay spirituality of service in the world. Beyond general outline and orientation, lay spirituality needs more specific development, especially regarding a daily program for leading a spiritual life and the modes of publicly witnessing Christian commitment.

Often lay people are given a watered-down version of a convent or seminary spiritual program. With a wife or husband and small children as essential parts of one's daily life, a monastic regularity of lengthy prayer will never work, and can actually impede the apostolic charism of prayer and service that is being offered to these lay people. But these people, especially former religious, tend to think the spiritual program of religious life is the only one available. And when it does not work, they feel frustrated and helpless. Some creative experimenting with the traditional means for spiritual growth is needed by lay people, in dialogue with people experienced in spirituality, to find the specifics for married people of an active apostolic spiritual program, which will encompass every detail of their daily lives and help them know and trust God's love in all.

Since lay people, far more than is still usual for most religious and priests, will be deeply committed in the public arena of our world, they will face difficult questions about how to witness to their Christian commitment in the work world, and about how to respond to issues like nuclear disarmament, strike possibilities, energy conservation, consumerism, rising unemployment, erosion of family values and stability, and many others. Lay people will have to respond to these issues somehow just because of where and how they live their lives. How can they be helped to respond prayerfully, in the light of the whole Christian revelation, and not be left just to do the best they can on their own?

Chapter Two

1981: SOME OVERARCHING THEMES
AND A FEW SPECIFICS

In the previous chapter I surveyed the currents in the ebb and flow of the past decade of the stream of American spirituality. This chapter looks again, one year later, at movements within that stream, the stream of Christian spirituality in this country as it moves toward the close of the twentieth century. The stream is anything but stagnant, and so the year's flow has made a difference. Some of the currents run deep and provide a depth of clarity in the stream. Other currents are strong but close to the surface and so they conceal, at least for now, any depth of clarity. Still other movements within the stream are cloudy and muddy, and prevent any clear predictions about themselves. However, it remains instructive and fascinating and, hopefully, inspiring to reflect again upon the stream of American spirituality.

This chapter will relate directly and substantively to the previous one, and in many ways. Obviously, as a reflection just one year later, it will be more limited than the last chapter's review of an entire decade. Further, because almost all the issues of the decade covered in that chapter remain very much with us, this chapter presupposes and reaffirms many issues previously presented. I must settle for the last chapter's treatment of many of the issues or run the risk of too much duplication. For this reason the deci-

43

sion not to repeat various issues does not imply that
the questions are settled or are any less alive and tan-
talizing. Some of what follows is a new and more
thorough treatment of previous issues, while in other
parts I am developing entirely new issues that have
surfaced this year in my experience and reading. And
as was true in the previous chapter, my goal here is
neither to prioritize nor to resolve issues, but rather to
describe and develop them in a way that focuses them
for the reader's own further reflection and development. Finally, this chapter is divided differently than
the previous one. I treat at some length four over-
arching themes and then more briefly present eight
subordinate concerns reflected in today's American
spiritual scene.

I. FOUR FUNDAMENTAL CONCERNS

Among the deeper desires of the human heart,
we find four very fundamental issues: love, joy, companionship, and enthusiasm. These basic desires of
the heart lie behind four overarching issues in
American spirituality today. Each of these issues can
be stated in the form of a separate question: 1. Must
true human love and encouragement move toward a
relationship that is deeper than immediate sensual expression and that is more permanent than a brief,
passing affair? 2. Is the joy and profound happiness
of self-discovery finally a matter of self-love and self-
concern—or of self-oblation? 3. How do we achieve a
true union of minds and hearts in a shared faith-
vision? 4. How can we sustain a realistic enthusiasm
in the midst of our disturbing, unpredictable world?

Though I will treat each of these basic themes separately, there is certainly much fruitful, overlapping implication among them.

1. Profound and Faithful Love. The sensual immediacy of an instant fix is blatant among the affective ideals of our culture. Upon even the most cursory examination, TV talk shows, movies, novels and advertising reveal both the conscious and the subliminal dominance of this ideal. We are invited to expect that love, encouragement, sympathy, acceptance be experiences that are *felt,* and felt instantly, in one night, one weekend, one workshop, one interpersonal encounter. And so permanence, perseverance and patient profundity are replaced by the transient, the disposable, the intensely superficial. Love as a relationship that matures only slowly and patiently, and which becomes in any way fully itself only as it moves toward the permanence of fidelity, has at best a perilous footing in modern consciousness. Some of the denials of the permanence and profundity of love are indeed very explicit, but the more insidious erosion of love is its subliminal limitation by our culture to a matter of immediate stimulation and satisfaction. As with the air we breathe, most of us are unaware of the prevalence of this diminishment of love. And so we rarely confront and react against its insidious influence.

Such a pervasive cultural message is going to have an enormous, harmful impact on spirituality. The recent reaction in spirituality, in itself legitimate, against a past, overly platonic stress on relationships that did not attend enough to the role of feelings and affectivity in true love, plays right into the cultural

45

stress on the intensely sensual and immediate aspects of love. Yet the intensity of immediate stimulation and the profundity of our core self are and will always be two really related experiences, but also really distinct, and often really different, experiences. Sensual intensity and love's profound spiritual center engage very different levels of the human person. Of course, rather than choosing between these two qualities of human experience, as if between a good and an evil, we must learn to recognize and evaluate each type of experience for the goodness each can be when integrated within the unified identity of our person. This is what human development is all about. A past denial of the role of an unpredictable sensuality in the process of human spiritual growth is just as misleading as the present cultural overstress on the immediate satisfaction of intense sensuality.

For the person of faith, the integration of sensual intensity and of profundity is an important area of spiritual discernment. The daily work of growth toward spiritual maturity is precisely the evaluation and direction of affective impulses such as joy, anger, envy, lust—an evaluation and direction that must be done in the light of God's love, a love which is profoundly alive in every human person's core identity. In this view, our transient, unpredictable sensuality is never taken as its own measure, its own norm. Rather it is evaluated and dealt with in the light of our core identity in faith. In this way affective impulses, properly dealt with, become an important means to spiritual maturity and to a deeper core identity before God in Christ Jesus. This process of evaluation and integration, which always requires graced insight, is for the spiritually mature person not a matter of cold, calculating logic but of an almost instantaneous sense, an intuition given in the midst of experience. But such a discerning sense results only from patient training in taking God's love ever more seriously. It is surely not given with birth.

The serious role of discernment in growth to spiritual adulthood is denied by our culture's insidious stress on the immediately intense satisfaction of sensual love. To confuse the distinction between the affectively transient and the profoundly core parts of the human person, and effectively to deny the profound permanence of which human love is capable, is to short-circuit and, finally, to destroy genuine spiritual maturity.

Celibate love relationships, of course, are also susceptible of harmful cultural influence. Appropriate love relationships with others, though increasingly popular among celibates, are not easy to manage well today. Some celibates shrink from genuinely affective involvement, while others, at times unreflectively, are led into intense, emotional relationships which later on either reveal themselves to be in violation of celibacy or end by being preferred as more satisfying than celibacy. I am in no way implying here that celibacy does or should segregate a person from love relationships with other human beings. Indeed, celibacy demands love relationships, love relationships of many kinds. But without a prayerful intimacy with God and a careful, decisive discernment of affective impulses, as briefly described above, the celibate can either remain infantile and undeveloped or can move into relationships that con-

47

fuse, and even violate the basic identity. It is illusion to think that every affective impulse in our consciousness will simply naturally be in line with and promote our celibate maturity. Such impulses must be evaluated and the evaluation must take place in the light of the permanent faith identity involved in a celibate vocation. It can be no surprise that the immediate satisfaction of a temporary, sensual love is surely different from, and may well, at least initially and where recollection is weak, appear more attractive than the deep but quiet satisfaction of heart of the celibate faith relationship with God—especially if the celibate person has failed to develop an appropriate sensual dimension in that relationship with God. In reaction to the cultural stress on intense, instant, sensual love, the celibate person needs a prayerful intimacy that makes possible a discernment which can integrate all the impulses and experiences of life into that profound, developing identity where permanent fidelity to God resides.

Family life as well as celibacy has been seriously harmed by the insidious cultural view of love and instant sensual satisfaction. The present sorry state of the family in this country is an almost predictable result of a transient "culture of the disposable," with its loss of respect for fidelity and permanence in love. The Year of the Family brought investigations of all sorts, including the summer White House Conference on the Family and the Synod of Bishops in Rome. But there is little sign of much change nationally. It is an issue being written about from many perspectives: educational,[1] economic,[2] moral,[3] among others.

The stable family, the fundamental building block of a healthy society, is disintegrating right before our eyes. It is a problem of immense proportions, and it challenges all Christians—lay, religious and priests—not just husbands, wives and children. A permanence of love, love that perseveres to the joy of ever deeper self-discovery in an identity shared with and in God, must withstand our culture's sensational view of trivialized love. But this cultural tide will not be easily turned, for we are talking here of an attitude which is influenced by highly complex factors in our society and by forces more powerfully influential than we easily realize. We are dealing, then, with an issue fraught with most serious spiritual implications, one that calls for both a serious analysis of, and a profound healing of, the roots of our society.

2. A More Refined Christian Personalism. Among other influences, Vatican II's articulation of the rediscovered value of Christian personalism has led to a change in many decision-making processes within the Church. Because of the greater stress placed on personal freedom and responsibility, individuals may make many more decisions for themselves. And they have much more in-put into decisions others make. For the most part, this has been a healthy development and has enriched the Church and many human lives. But we are ready now, I think, to take another step toward a more refined understanding of Christian personalism. Over the past years, reflection on our experience has taught us that genuine personalism can easily slip into a real, if often subtle and unintentional, selfishness. Basic self-love and self-acceptance, always crucial for healthy human maturity, if it becomes too self-conscious and dominant in a person's motivation, finally destroys the Christian ideal of personhood.

In his book, *Psychology as Religion,* Paul C. Vitz argues "that psychology has become a religion, in particular, a form of secular humanism based on worship of the self."[4] He criticizes Erich Fromm, Carl Rodgers, Abraham Maslow and Rollo May as four proponents of this selfist psychology-religion.[5] And he shows how pervasively this self-worship theory has moved into our culture. "In short, humanistic selfism is not a science but a popular secular substitute religion, which has nourished and spread today's widespread cult of self-worship."[6] Its pervasiveness is what makes it so insidious. It is in the air, and we breathe it into our bloodstream far more than we realize. Vitz's book, perhaps occasionally exaggerated or simplistic but overall very insightful and provocative, ends on a note that is hopeful and challenging for the Christian religion. "In another ten years, millions of people will be bored with the cult of the self and looking for a new life. The uncertainty is not the existence of this coming wave of returning prodigals, but whether their Father's house, the true faith, will still be there to welcome and celebrate their return."[7] For Christians, the response cannot simply be a dogged refusal to be contaminated by the selfist religion. Rather, our active grappling with the pervasiveness of this perhaps initially attractive but shallow and false substitute can reveal a call to greater, more selfless generosity—and this can only enrich the impact of Christianity in our world.

For the Christian, life is finally not self-love and self-worship. It is self-oblation in loving service to further the praise and worship of God in the beauty of Jesus. Healthy self-love never becomes an end in itself nor the motivating force in Christian decision. Jesus' words about self-discovery as rooted in self-oblation[8] are the very foundation for the Christian version of human development and of the way to true joy and happiness. For the healthy, humble person, self-fulfillment is never the conscious pursuit. Maturing in the spiritual life therefore is a continuing conversion, whereby we reject the subtle selfishness that life reveals as pervasive in us all. And in this way the self, as God intends and loves it—the humanity and originality and holiness of each of us—progressively occurs.

The issue I am raising here springs from another comment of Vitz: "Although the enthusiasm for selfism has probably begun to wane already, a whole generation has been deeply influenced by it."[9] I believe this is true. There are many good, generous people in the Church who have been raised and educated, more than they realize, in this selfist religion. Consequently, their important apostolic choices are now often very subtly, unconsciously, but very really, influenced by elements of this selfist perspective. Evidence of such an influence can be too central a focusing on issues like: what will be best for *me*, what will *I* enjoy most, what will help *me* grow most. Let me not be misunderstood. I am not referring here to that obvious self-centeredness which those same conscious, striving Christians would clearly recognize and usually attempt to reject. And I am certainly not denying the serious respect we should have for the gifts of individuals. Nor do I wish at all to discourage the profound joy that should most often inspire and flow from our apostolic choices and actions. But I am suggesting that the genuine growth and development of the past few years may allow us now to recognize and to screen out, with greater refinement of discernment, any subliminal selfist influence in our choices—and in this way to surrender to our loving God with ever more unambiguous clarity of heart and spirit. Such a radical yes requires great faith. But it will thereby give and reveal that gospel joy which Jesus knew in his surrender to his Father. And it will render our apostolic choices and efforts ever more united and effective in furthering that dream of justice of our Father which Jesus loved so fully and for which he worked so hard—even unto death.

3. *A Shared Companionship in Faith.* In every workshop I was involved with this past year, there were questions about community. Community. It is a subject most of us are very, very tired of hearing or talking about. But it remains a reality our hearts still long for. On all levels of Church membership this longing is evident: between husbands and wives; within families; within parish communities of pastor, curate, religious and laity; and among members of religious communities.

Many religious congregations feel a quiet sadness due to a lack of shared vision sufficient to bind the minds and hearts of their members together for zealous service. The confusion of basically different orientations to the vows in a community is one very essential matter that can preclude unity. The distinction between monastic and active spiritualities that I referred to in the previous chapter[10] leads to different orientations to the vows—and indeed to almost everything. Since clarity about this distinction among different spiritualities—a classic question—has only recently been fully addressed once again, the implications of the distinction in terms of the vows still need fuller insight and working out. As a result, both of these orientations to the vows—monastic apostolic and active apostolic—may exist in the same community, which can only cause confusion and even the threat of disharmony.

Active apostolic religious communities have their own concerns about community. Without desiring to slip into a monastic mode, a community questions how much physical presence of members is minimally required, if there is to be any meaningful union of minds and hearts among the members. On the local level, failure of members to spend enough time together in praying, in sharing their faith vision and in recreating together would seem to defy a union of minds and hearts. Of course, the requisite amount of this kind of presence cannot be legislated. It must be desired. But what are some of the means whereby we can call forth and channel this desire?

Father Pedro Arrupe, as Jesuit General Superior, in a talk to the Jesuit 31st General Congregation, spoke of a new art of governing and a new art of obeying today in religious life.[11] This new art of governing and obeying can promote a new union of minds and hearts in a shared vision. But if this new art is not appreciated and embodied in the whole group, it will then become not unifying but divisive and a source of tension. Many groups, I feel, have now overcome their reaction against any past, excessively domineering role of religious authority within a community and so they are ready now to appreciate genuine authority within community and to recognize it as a special servant of apostolic unity.[12] The theory of an accountability that is shared with the whole local community may seem good, but what are the concrete forms that will give flesh to such an accountability? How do we call forth the requisite courage and trust to share quite explicitly our faith vision, so that accountability is even feasible? And renewal that is not persisted in can actually prove a setback. After the inspiration of a planned experience of faith-sharing within a community, the pain of its absence over time is intensified. The style of a local community's life and conversation can become so secular that individual religious hearts become quietly but very really secularized, and the faith vision, rather than shared, corrodes. Well, these are just a few aspects of the very real concern abroad about religious life as a shared companionship in faith. And we avoid these questions and concerns only at the risk of frustrating fundamental human and religious desires and at the risk of dooming the future ministry of religious life in this country.

A parish should also provide support and a shared responsibility that is rooted in the faith vision of pastor, curates, religious and lay people. In some parishes there is development along this line. But in many parishes, there is very little such development.[13] And this causes frustration, and often dropouts in active membership. In many cases reconciliation is needed. But it will not be easy, because the causes of the problem are complicated and touch deeply the sensibilities of the people involved. But if all parties really desire the companionship that results from a shared vision of mission, and if they are humble enough to admit past mistakes, they can move slowly to the changes of attitude that would make the requisite reconciliation possible.

4. The Paschal Vision of a Realistic, Sustained Enthusiasm. Television, newspapers and magazines catalogue the latest daily or weekly version of this world's folly. Always a new example of unjust suffering and dying and of things going awry. Rather than improving, in many ways the state of our world seems to be getting worse. How do apostles, critically involved with this world, maintain an enthusiastic spirit? Burnout of spirit in discouragement and cynicism is frequent. Sometimes a person finds that only in the unrealistic seclusion of an escape from our real world can enthusiasm and hope be maintained. But this enthusiasm is chimerical, never stands the test of reality, and so is of no real use, certainly of no apostolic use, to anybody.

The issue is not simply a matter of greater personal satisfaction for the apostle. Of course, enthusiasm always feels better. But the issue cuts far deeper than that: an unenthusiastic witness of the Gospel is a countersign. We are talking of something profound—not about the temperament of a cheerleader. Genuine enthusiasm of spirit can only spring from a profound faith vision, from a life hidden with Christ in God. Active apostolic people in the Church perhaps especially feel this challenge for an enthusiasm of service that is fully involved in, but clearly rooted beyond and deeper than, their own shifting moods or the sorry state of our world. And the issue, finally, is apostolic. For it is not just a matter of the apostle's staying power. It is about the apostolically primary matter of witnessing effectively to a Father's loving power surprising his dying Son in the intimacy of Resurrection.

The maintained enthusiasm of a human heart radically depends upon an interior, sustained intimacy. Alienation and loneliness always disorient and militate against enthusiasm. The etymology of the word enthusiasm (en theos: in God) is right to the point. Only someone whose identity is rooted beyond this world "in God" is capable of sustained enthusiasm. Enthusiasm, of course, is a tough reality—by no means always accompanied by happy feelings or pleasure. The passion and death of Jesus reveals a whole new model of humanly experienced intimacy with God. All through the most horrible, unfair suffering of Jesus, he is sustained by the intimacy and power of his Father's loving care. In the moment of his dying, stripped of everything including his felt experience of being Son,[14] Jesus discovers anew the intimacy of his Father's loving care in Resurrection. The Resurrection reveals that never for a moment is he really without the intimacy of his Father's love. And so Jesus' experience promises a potential for all of us. In everything, including the most horrible and unjust suffering and dying, the enlivening intimacy of our God's loving care is available to each and everyone of us. Only in the light of this vision is enthusiasm realistic and possible for people deeply immersed apostolically in our world. The very suffering and dying of our world, never good in themselves, become elements, in light of

Jesus' experience, of the growth of that Kingdom of love and peace and justice of his Father.

Such a paschal vision, that can find enthusiasm in God even in the face of suffering and dying, is of course far more easily stated and described than lived. It takes time and patiently courageous discernment sufficiently to deepen this vision so that it genuinely enlightens all our daily service. And while this vision will never render our zeal complacent in the face of the injustices of our world, it will cause our zeal to be profoundly tempered by the enthusiastic patience of an invisible Father whose love and care far transcend our world—that world for which nevertheless his only Son died, because his Father loved it so much.

This issue of a realistic apostolic enthusiasm has another angle to it in the life of many religious communities. In the face of decreased numbers and increased apostolic needs, many discussions among religious reveal a heavy sadness and a lack of confidence. This discouragement is contagious, a pervasive desolation sapping the spirit of whole congregations. This is the opposite of enthusiasm. And often it results from facing the present situation of decreased numbers and increased apostolic need in an apparently too practical way—in a worldly, unspiritual way which is, in the long run and, from faith's point of view, a most impractical approach. Faith suggests a viewpoint based on the paschal vision revealed in Jesus' dying. If we have not profoundly confronted in the present situation the call to die and have not prayed for the freedom that comes in the surrender of dying into a loving God's hands, then a realistically enthusiastic and hopeful spirit simply is not possible. Many more religious, in congregations not dramatically facing extinction, must similarly read the present situation in a more deeply spiritual light, with a precious freedom born of the grace of the "charismatic art of dying."[15] A quietly pervasive desolation in many religious communities can only be dispelled by a freedom born in the face of death. Only in this way can apostolic planning be done enthusiastically, creatively, and with a realistic hope and trust in God's Spirit at work in a particular congregation.

II. SOME OTHER CONCERNS ON THE SPIRITUAL SCENE

Beyond these fundamental issues of a proper view of love, of a refined Christian personalism, of community and of enthusiasm, I will now treat more briefly a few other issues, among many that merit attention.

1. Moving Marginal People in Religious Life. In the decade or so immediately after Vatican II there was much experimentation, and people and projects were allowed to develop much more on their own than had been true in the past. These were exciting, adventurous years. But not always easy ones, for many religious found their lives thrown into confusion and a large number left religious life. All of this is hardly finished. We are still very much in process. But there is a lot more stability in many congregations. Those who remained have had to renew their original choice, have had to rededicate themselves to God in the spirit of the particular religious community to which they belong. And so there is perhaps a closer unity among many of the members, a unity born of a renewed understanding of religious life in the Church.

But in most congregations there are still people who are attitudinally marginated from the center of this renewed group. Oftentimes they happen to be by themselves, living outside community. They can be either progressive or reactionary, living either outside or within community. But what is important is that attitudinally they are very slightly, if at all, part of the community and its apostolic mission. Little of their person is invested in the identity of the congregation. These marginal people, now more than in the previous confusing period, sap the spirit of the renewed community. For this reason, these marginals must be helped to move. With utmost care and consideration, they should first be invited to rejoin the community. If that fails, they must be helped to move to what will be best for them and for the community.

This is happening in many congregations. It is difficult, and open to a facile misinterpretation. To exercise patient care of the marginal individual and yet to act on the clarity about religious life we now have is not easy for the person who has responsibility for taking such action. To move in this direction does not imply a narrow, overly uniform view of religious life, nor does it of itself call an end to any new, experimental developments for the future. Nor does it necessarily involve any failure to welcome the prophetic and creative in religious life. It is not uncommon to suggest that dealing compassionately but clearly with the marginated is a reactionary movement. But this is to misunderstand what is at issue, in most cases. Such action seeks to receive and incarnate

59

concretely the renewed if partial clarity of the present and to promote the renewed spirit of the congregation. Such accountability to the fruits of experiment and renewal is essential, if religious life is to move into its future with strength, for the greater service of the Church.

2. *Incarnating a Renewed Clarity.* Dealing with marginal people in religious life is only one specific instance of a more general phenomenon which perhaps warrants a separate listing. We are not now so confused and timid about the value and meaning of religious life as we were a few years back. And what attracts us about religious life today, while not a violent contradiction of the past, is certainly not simply a matter of "the same old thing." But many do enjoy a renewed clarity and a humble confidence we have not known for a while. Many congregations are treasuring this clarity by incarnating it in various forms, practices and structures in the community's life. What had become vague and loose is now specified and more precisely pointed in the desired direction. Formation programs, while respecting the variety of human development, have re-introduced structures and practices which facilitate the radical reorientation in faith of a person according to the religious charism of the community. Programs in preparation for final profession both spell out signs that evidence necessary maturity for permanent fidelity and provide specific helps to discern and nurture sufficient growth and permanence in a vocation.

Just as in the treatment of marginal people, this trend should not be misinterpreted. It can seem to be a return to old structures and practices which, some would claim, should never have been discarded. To allow such a cynical misunderstanding could serve a type of reactionary backlash and be dangerous for the future.

What I see happening in this trend is a definite move into the future, and not a return to the past. Something new is being implemented. If practices of the past, in many cases valuable for that past age, had not been discarded, we would not now be moving closer to a new vision of religious life. Even when a newly implemented practice looks similar to an older one, a renewed understanding of that practice allows a different use and accomplishment. This new vision of religious life is attempting to incarnate itself in a contemporary expression of a profound rootedness in God that always produces a greater flexibility in future service.

The following trend is another aspect of this more general phenomenon I have considered here.

3. Rewriting Constitutions. Many congregations are in the midst of the tedious but important process of rewriting constitutions. The fifteen years of renewal and experimentation since Vatican II have provided plenty of material for a carefully discerning reflection. And this discerning reflection now allows for, and calls for, a renewed description, in new constitutions, of the congregation's identity, spirit, way of life and apostolic mission.

There should be clarity about the kind of statement intended by constitutions. Though they are always open to revision and updating, constitutions are not a temporary document of minor importance. Hence, they should not be expressed in a manner so topical and contemporary that they are quickly out of date. On the other hand, neither should they be so general that they are vague—nor so juridical and canonical that they are spiritually uninspiring. They should be a document that, in almost any age, inspires prayer, that stirs the members' hearts. As everyone has learned, the preparatory work is as important as the work of the general chapter which finalizes the new document. The process of prayerful reflection and dialogue within the whole congregation not only taps the fruits of the Spirit of each person but also involves everybody in a way that allows the promulgation of the final version to be an experience of renewed unity, inspiration and apostolic vigor in the congregation.[16]

Some congregations are experiencing serious difficulties as they conclude this process of rewriting constitutions. The reform of new constitutions does not guarantee the renewal of heart and spirit of the individual members. Follow-up processes on the local level, to help members assimilate the new constitutions, are necessary to help incarnate reformed constitutions in the hearts and minds of a particular congregation. Some congregations are having trouble getting their new constitutions approved by Rome. Sometimes this is due to terminological differences, rather than to any profoundly different views of religious life. In other cases, when it does go beyond words to different views of vowed active apostolic religious life, it is hard for a religious congregation to have adequate communication with Rome, in order to share the urgency of the specific local issue or setting in the world which is determining the new and different viewpoint. Since the rewriting of constitutions is such an important process for the future of religious life in the Church, one would hope that the process is never rushed to an unsatisfactory conclusion, that the channels of communication with Rome are open and adequate, and that one specific mentality is not allowed to evaluate new proposals according to a too narrowly univocal and uniform view and expression of religious life. Not apart from, but together with a thorough sense of tradition and its development over the years, there is needed a spiritual insight to recognize the contemporary development and expression of religious life.

4. Daily Liturgy. In the past, daily Mass was taken as a standard sign of the seriousness of someone's spiritual life. Religious always went to daily Mass. Then Vatican II gave much of the liturgical renewal public ecclesiastical approval and effected very specific changes in our way of worship and prayer. There is now, I feel, a change in the daily Mass habit. And though I focus my comments here on religious life, this issue extends far beyond religious. Almost ten years ago there was a fair amount of discussion about, and some rebellion against, the practice of daily liturgy.[17] Then that died down. Now it is not openly talked of much, but many people have slipped into, if they have not chosen, patterns other than daily eucharistic celebration. Prayerful reflection, consultation and discussion of the following questions might help insure a person's choice about one or other pattern as preferable. How central a role does the liturgy play in keeping the consciousness of busy apostolic people religiously focused? Together with many daily apostolic experiences, can the liturgy be a privileged moment of recollection each day for Christian apostolic consciousness? Is it simply a matter of getting more work done if time is saved from a daily liturgy? Is there a sense in which different styles of liturgy allow a daily celebration of our faith fitted to the liturgical quality of the day? What different styles are now suggested in the approved liturgical norms and directives, and what further variety should be permitted? How available is "good" liturgy without at the same time expecting something far ahead of the general, and especially the local, community of the Church? How often should the local religious community gather for its own liturgy to promote its spiritual unity? Underneath all these questions is the need, in a rapidly secularizing world, to celebrate our experienced faith vision so as to keep our heart and apostolic efforts affectively focused in a Father's forgiving love, never more attractively revealed than in a Son's faithful dying to Resurrection. Many of these questions are not easily answered, but facing up to them could be a rich stimulus for spiritual growth and could avoid the possibility of slipping into a pattern of eucharistic practice which would not really respond to, or improve, our religious consciousness and apostolic zeal.

5. Respect for Papal Leadership. From his election there were some dramatic aspects of the papacy of John Paul II. As time passes there are other ways in which his papacy differs from that of his two predecessors. He seems to know what he wants. And he is speaking his mind, with a precise clarity, on a wide range of moral topics about which, in recent years, there has been some confusion and disagreement within the ranks of the Church. His philosophical background allows him to analyze our world and to write glowingly of the Christian dimensions of human existence. He is geographically bringing the papacy to the faithful all over the world. His robust, enthusiastic presence has a charm and a great, charismatic appeal wherever he goes.

But as time goes on, parts of the Church are not finding it easy to receive Pope John Paul II. Combined within his person are a charm and electric magnetism before groups, an apparent moral and doctrinal conservatism,[18] and a passionate concern for the poor and for social justice. Some have written him off completely, whether with a casual or a sad disregard, while others choose to respect some parts of his leadership and to disregard other parts. Some are enthused at his social concerns but disregard his other moral and doctrinal stands. Some are easily excited by the magnetism of his personal presence—his media qualities—but quite simply disregard his opinions on anything. Some wonder whether he is speaking too quickly and out of a narrow, nationalistic background, rather than taking the trouble to inform himself carefully of more universal perspectives before he enunciates any clear opinions—much less decisions. To many, then, in some ways his leadership is exciting and in others it is disappointing.

We have not wrestled enough with this issue of respect for John Paul II's leadership in the Church. There has not been time enough yet to understand what God is saying to the Church in the person of this complicated man. It is an issue to be faced, for Peter is part of the mystery of Christ. Facing the issue will involve a serious, carefully integrating, respectful study of John Paul's speeches and writings, if we are to come to a genuine, profound respect for his leadership in the Church.[19] But these concerns must be studied while praying for greater faith—a faith which makes use of all ordinary, human, subtle means of interpreting his words, a faith which takes advantage of the ordinary channels to keep the ranks of the Church in dialogue with him, and a faith which seriously reverences his leadership—even while avoiding any exaggerated deifying of his person and authority in the Church. In this way he may gradually become, as the holder of the petrine office always should be, a source of genuine, growing, graced unity in the whole Church.

Somewhere in all of this there is a call to live our faith existentially, in the form of an appropriate, intelligent respect and reverence for the personal leadership of the man whom God has given us as Jesus' vicar in the Church. There may be insecurity about what the future of John Paul II's papacy may bring. But we are asked to trust, not in a mindless, inhuman way, but with a spirit that springs from great belief and love of our Father and his dream of justice—that dream which Jesus revealed, and lived—and is.

6. Priestly Spirituality. The issue of the spirituality of priests, mentioned in the previous chapter,[20] continues as an issue facing the Church in her own renewal. Obviously, the need for increased prayer and spiritual growth touches all of us—and very much, therefore, all priests. But I choose to focus here on the issue as it touches the diocesan priesthood. It goes without saying how enormously influential parish priests are. To treat the issue of their spirituality, therefore, is to touch upon something with far-reaching effects throughout the whole community of the Church.

Though there undoubtedly continues to be growth among diocesan priests in the practice of prayer, I sense that a great need remains. In some dioceses support groups of priests provide encouragement and stimulus for prayer and spiritual growth. At the same time there may remain an attitude which inhibits mature spiritual seriousness. I personally believe, from my limited experience in priests' retreats and workshops, that some very fundamental changes may be called for if the prayerful quality of priestly life is to grow. Serious study and reflection on this issue may be in order—something to be done by diocesan priests themselves, perhaps, with the help of people trained in spirituality.

Some seminaries do not seem to succeed in training to a spiritual seriousness by inculcating habits of personal responsibility for frequent, regular, formal prayer. Other places present a type of prayer program which may well be unrealistic for a busy priest's future life. In still other situations, a young priest is sometimes hard put to withstand the subtle, but very real and strong, peer pressure against a seriously developing prayer life.

As has always been true, it is easy for the busy person to escape into a daily round of vocal prayer that, after a while, touches little of the mind and heart. To avoid this escape, a priest needs, beyond the vocal prayer of the liturgy of the Hours, some regular affective prayer of presence in faith before God as the Beloved of his celibate heart. Priests' annual retreats seem so often to have an expectation and custom which turn them into social reunions, which serve a very real, indeed essential, but very different value, but which prevents the kind of interior silence necessary for a profound experience of God in prayer. I surely do not mean to place blame here. Rather, the problem seems to lie with structures in the early years of training, structures not easy to revamp, but which have resulted in certain attitudes and expectations.

If diocesan priests were to deal with some of these problems, various good effects may occur. The quality of parish homilies would surely be affected, and the growing number of disaffected, educated faithful, who often seem to find so little help in the parish homily, will be served.[21] The good busy lives most priests lead would be even more effective for God, and their personal lives would be more inspiringly simple and joyful. This might also make more possible the cooperation and teamwork needed so much among priests and people in parish life. At last year's Bishops' Synod in Rome, Mother Teresa saw a relationship between holy priests and the quality of family life when she told the bishops, "If you want to do something for families, give us holy priests."[22]

As discussion of the feasibility of married priests continues, it seems very important that a pervasive spiritual renewal of the diocesan priesthood be undertaken before any serious consideration is given to married priests. Marriage, of itself, will certainly not bring holiness to the priesthood. It should be the other way around: the experience of a prayerfully renewed diocesan priesthood in the Church should precede any final serious deliberation about a married clergy.

Surely a bishop all by himself can never resolve the problem of the spiritual renewal of his priests. But it is hard to overstress the value of bishops who are pastoral theologians with a trained, contemporary, spiritual sensitivity.

7. Priests and Politics. This past year Father Robert Drinan, a Jesuit priest and congressman, announced he was not running for re-election. Through his Jesuit superior, he had been ordered by the Pope to remove himself from Congress. Father Drinan's difficult but obedient response was an inspiration to many, as attested by personal letters to him from Father Arrupe, as Jesuit Superior General and from his own provincial superior in New England. But this case, because of its publicity, has stirred some heated discussion within the Church. It has raised questions and occasioned some doubtful conclusions.

Some confusion on the issue may be due to the fact that there has been no formal explanation of the rationale behind the Pope's order. I have heard some claim that the Pope meant to say that faith should have nothing to do with politics and that Christians should not be involved in politics. This would be hard to square with many of the Pope's own very strong statements at Puebla and in Brazil. To suggest that faith and politics don't relate would be a simple falsification of the mind of John Paul II. As far as we can tell, it was precisely a publicly elected political office that the Pope did not want a priest to hold. To run for election a priest must be publicly associated with the ideology of a political party—and in such a way, many would feel, that his ability to preach God's Word in the liturgy could be compromised, if not destroyed. He would always be open to the insinuation, at least, that his political ideology was unduly coloring his preaching of God's Word. So the decision of the Pope may perhaps be seen as an effort to protect all priests' power to preach the Word, not apart from, but beyond, any particular, party ideology.

There are a number of other questions which, at this point, do not seem to be involved. A priest can be politically involved in ways other than elected office. And the Pope's concern, as presently known, seems to be with priests, not religious or lay persons. Indeed, there is a great need for deeply Christian believers to be intimately involved in politics, so that Christian values may have appropriate influence there. Much of this could change with further words or actions on Pope John Paul's part.

It would seem, then, that one specific point was made by Pope John Paul II in the Drinan affair. That point should not be exaggerated, nor should it discourage us in our passionate pursuit of God's justice in our world. Hopefully, it will stimulate serious study about many other ways that Christian faith not only can, but must be expressed and lived by all of us, including priests, in the very influential, essential human task which politics is. And we have not just the Drinan affair to spur on such serious study and action about how we may all be involved in politics in a suitable way. The growing roll call of martyrs for justice in Latin America and around the world is a loud, clear summons.

8. Sexist Language About God. The issue of the use of sexist language in referring to God can be seen as one aspect of an issue developed in the previous chapter: the role of women in the world and the Church. Without repeating myself, I want, and only very tentatively, to acknowledge this issue—a matter with which we will struggle more and more in the coming years. I find it especially difficult here to predict any likely outcomes.

This issue, somehow involved with the correction of a past discrimination against women, can never finally be resolved simply in terms of women's rights. Some profound spiritual and scriptural questions invite the serious, prayerful investigation of trinitarian theologians. Is Jesus' addressing Yahweh as *Abba* simply and totally the expression of a first-century hebrew, male-dominated culture? Does *Abba* reveal and promise a human intimacy of religious experience beyond the masculine or feminine? Is there a twentieth-century equivalent which does not destroy the religious intimacy of Jesus' *Abba*—neither within his experience nor within our own?

I sense there are many women, sensitive to the issue of women's rights, who are experiencing the qualities of intimacy revealed in Jesus and are not bothered by Jesus' masculine reference to God. However, the issue will not easily disappear. As we strive to take it seriously, there may be some strong reactions, since a new linguistic style of reference, never simply a trade for an older style without affecting basic meaning, can upset a long tradition about such a deeply personal reality as God.[23] But happily the effort will also lead us to a greater purification of our image of the rich transcendence of the one true

God, so far beyond both masculine and feminine—the One who is more personal than any and all human reality, the One who is utter mystery—the One in whom alone each of us finds fulfillment. Maybe a year of careful listening will provide more clarity.

Chapter Three

1982: TRENDS AND ISSUES
IN A SECULARIZING WORLD

I. INTRODUCTORY REMARKS

When you think of it, the year 1981-82, even viewed coldly, was startling. And yet, how fearfully accustomed, and how quickly forgetful, we become. We heard—and saw—assassination attempts on President Reagan and Pope John Paul II; the ecstasy, after 444 days of agony, of the freeing of the hostages from Tehran; the on-going murders in Central America; the endless floods of refugees throughout the world, in Central America, Africa, Thailand; the persistent, "small-scale wars," fully sufficient to keep alive the fear and plausibility of World War III; the continually escalating number of divorces and abortions across this land of ours; and those few, terrifying nuclear missile mistakes that accompanied the deliberate, quite unmistaken increase of nuclear armaments on the part of the major world powers—and minor powers, too. These events warn both author and reader that life is fragile—and that it may be viewed as very cheap; that evil is very real—and that we may easily get numb to its great, dark mystery; and that faith in God as a search for meaning and as love of the reality of our world is not easy—not easy at all.

Once again the contents of this chapter will build on the developments treated in the previous two chapters because spiritual trends and issues ordinarily do not simply appear and vanish within the narrow purview of a single year. And certainly, for this reader of the signs of the times, the four fundamental concerns of the last chapter continue to be of paramount importance for all personal and communal spiritual life in the church today: concern for the possibility of a profound and faithful love, in the face of our culture's penchant for sensational, dramatic, immediate—and short-lived—sensual stimulation; concern for a more refined, a more other-centered, Christian personalism; concern for a shared companionship in faith; and concern for the paschal character and quality of faith, a paschal faith requisite to sustain, for the long haul, realistic, apostolic enthusiasm.[1] Indeed, because the cultural influences at work in these four areas of concern are still very strong, this present chapter will relate to them in many ways.

As I have travelled about, consulted, read, given workshops, courses, retreats and spiritual direction this past year, a very dominant, over-arching preoccupation and theme, for me—as I reflect on my own experience and listen to the experience of others—is secularity, secularization, secularim. Human spiritual life exists only in a world where ongoing pressures come at us, from every side, to secularize all our experience—of ourselves, of one another, and of all aspects of our world. Certainly, there is nothing new about this observation. The matter has been with us for a century, and more. And in very current forms, it has been an overt preoccupation of the religious community in this country at least since Vatican II. But I believe that its strength as a trend in serious spiritual life continues very much to grow. And so, after looking about me, I have chosen to reflect here, at considerable length, on this tendency toward secularization. Following that, I will more briefly, discuss a number of trends and issues which, whether implicitly or explicitly, whether as cause or consequence or corollary, relate to this central trend of secularization. In general, as I treat these other trends and issues, I will leave to the reflection of the reader their precise relationship to the general theme of secularization.

II. SECULARIZATION

It is not uncommon to divide reality into the sacred and the secular. And though this distinction and its significance can be of immense subtlety and complication, with serious traps for the unwary, we can attempt a simple, hopefully usable description here of these two aspects of reality. John Coleman, using Huston Smith, makes the distinction for us:

> By the "secular" I mean "regions of life that man understands and controls, not necessarily completely but . . . for all practical purposes." These are regions toward which humans adopt a basically utilitarian attitude of mastery and control, making judgments on the basis of the technical adequacy of means to achieve stipulated goals.[2]

So the secular speaks to a world of human domination, understanding and control without, at least, any *necessary* reference to God or appeal to, or nourishment from, the experience of faith or of religious affections. Coleman then describes the sacred:

> By the "sacred" I mean the area of mystery—the incomprehensible, indomitable, and seriously and supremely important; for "the sacred exceeds not only our control but our comprehension." Our characteristic attitudes toward the sacred are all celebration, participatory contemplation, and gratitude rather than mastery.[3]

So the sacred points to the reverently mysterious, the awesomely (not problematically) uncontrollable and, for articulated Christian belief, to a living, personal, experienced relationship with God in faith and hope and love.

The tendency toward secularization in a world of human believers is inevitable. And it may foster religious faith—or it may corrupt it. The human heart, in this world, however lofty and transcendent its desires may be, is, ought to be, always historical, definite, incarnational. However much travel and communication have mobilized us, limitations of space and time still shape our identity. These limits can seem very restrictive and confining. To live in America or Poland or Iran as the 20th century closes may seem a paltry destiny, when compared with the space address that may well be among the options of our 23rd-century descendants. But these temporal and spatial limits to identify us now and, rather than confining us, can call forth those precise creative responses which will bring about the reality of space living in the future. As human realities, faith and religion must be planted and grow within this world. And so, they too are susceptible to time/space limitations. Though faith will always call us beyond the world, its healthy development always lies in vigorous interaction with the world and its daily round of activities. Spirituality is never simply faith—but rather, it is faith's interaction with culture. It therefore grows and incarnates itself precisely through a secularizing process and trend. With its central focus on Jesus of Nazareth, and therefore on incarnation, Christian spirituality not only tolerates but embraces, for the sake of its own existence and development, this secularizing interaction with the culture of a specific people and time.

And this secularizing process can positively foster faith, because the Kingdom of his Father which Jesus preached and lived, for the people of first century Palestine, was meant to be lived in the world. In his parables, Jesus took illustrations from the culture of ordinary people, and he challenged everyone to a whole new way of imagining life in this universe. Granted that the fullness of his Father's Kingdom beckoned beyond all this here and now, still the Kingdom became an illusion if it did not take flesh in the daily circumstances of a specific culture. Over these 20 centuries, the continually limited situation of human faith has successively called for multiple creative responses in the spirit—responses that lead to developments of both dogma and Christian life and that transform aspects of cultures, as each response incarnates, just a bit more, that loving Reign of his Father which Jesus so desired for all. Though it is not always easy to interpret what is or is not providential, history is of course also dotted with instances of mistaken, or at least very tardy, responses of the Church to certain cultural challenges.

Speaking summarily, then, we must be careful not to interpret the inevitable trend toward secularization as, of itself, destructive or weakening of Christian faith and witness. There is a healthy, permanent, indispensable secularity to Jesus' vision of loving and trusting his Father.

However, having spoken to the essential character of its positive meaning and purpose, we must frankly notice that this inevitable secularizing tendency, when not carefully purified and focused, can be dangerously corrupting of the life of faith. And we are speaking here of no mere danger, it seems to me, but of an actual trend of significant strength. The secularizing tendency of life in our world can and does easily, both consciously and unconsciously, settle into secularism, as an overall view of reality. John Coleman helps us again, this time quoting Guy Swanson:

> Secularism is the "denial that sacred order exists, the conviction that the universe is in no meaningful sense an expression or embodiment of purpose, the belief that it is unreasonable, other than anthropomorphically, to have toward the universe or its 'ground' a relationship mediated by communication or by any other interchange of meanings—to have toward it a relationship in any sense interpersonal."[4]

In this view, the world has become all, has become the ultimate: it has become God. Here we are entirely beyond any secularity, any inevitable and useful tendency toward secularization. As a vision of all reality, secularism has no time for faith, no basis for faith—much less for the intimacy of all true religion's interpersonal relationship with God.

In any explicit debate about secularism, of course, this corrupting danger for faith can be clearly perceived—and so the option to reject it is very available. But even at the theoretical, or notional, level, rejection is not so easy, when the inroads are far advanced. However, it is at the *operative* level, the lived level, the level of heart and eyes and hands, where the danger is especially insidious, and much less detectable—in the midst of our busy, unreflecting life.

The human heart, I believe, is essentially religious, with desires and longings for an interpersonal intimacy that far exceed anything and everything that is of this world. And often, by God's grace, a resentful, depressing frustration results when our hearts settle for less than all that they are made for. But the sensationally sensual immediacy of much of the affective revolution occurring in our world can fixate our hearts and distract them from a reverential love of God.[5] As the technological explosion more and more shapes our world, and as we, often rightly, professionally train for work that is more overtly secular, there can be less talk and reference to what should also be religious—even overtly religious. Letters, conversations—sometimes, even, participation in religious ceremonies—cease to involve any personal religious expression. I do not mean to imply here that religious faith is adequately, or even chiefly, measured by overt God-talk. But to keep the basic faith relationship of our hearts alive and growing, we surely need more than academic precision and culturally sophisticated reserve when expressing our faith. Faith, as a deep vision of heart, must be regularly expressed with appropriate personal devotion and affection. Otherwise, the vision and personal relationship of faith will, at minimum, lose any serious motivational force for our lives. It may even become something we are actually ashamed of. And when this happens—when our life of faith and devotion becomes entirely privatized, it can escape into a childish, uncritical pietism, because so rarely shared with anyone.

But there is a third, more ominous possibility. Our faith, from lack of expression, from lack of embodiment, may actually die. This is obviously serious—and it is often final—when a person's love relationship with God in Jesus loses all power, all effect in furthering his loving justice in our oppressively unjust world. And there is nothing theoretical in this very inadequate thumbnail sketch. Are there any readers who have not watched, in themselves or in a friend, as faith weakened in a movement from a growing silence regarding faith to an indifference or even an aggressive criticism, until every expression of faith has become uncomfortable and unwelcome. Then, faith no longer plays a role either in choosing or in evaluating action.

In a rapidly secularizing world, the possibility is very real that faith may harden into a cold, polite, sophisticated, professional stance to life, with very little warmly affective religious expression. But we always need to talk about our beloved with others, to keep the love affair alive and growing and to let it influence others. Appropriate personal expressions of our faith will usually serve the Holy Spirit's inspiration of others. And therefore Christian communities of every kind, whether in religious life, or the family, or the parish, become increasingly more valuable as supports of shared religious vision and experience within a world tending more and more to secularism.

How can we avoid the ultimate denial of Christian faith that secularism is? One terribly important means is surely that on-going faith experience which knows, and seeks to experience God as beyond and greater than all the world. We who can so easily shrink God and conveniently fit him into our small universe have Jesus himself, in his experience of his Father, as our example in this matter. As he came to know Yahweh of the Old Testament in his own growing *Abba* experience, Jesus related most personally to a God whose life and love neither depended on nor were equal to this world, though (and here is the adventure of it) Jesus himself *was* that Father's inextricable involvement in love with this world. His commitment to a God so far transcending, though intimately involved within, this world is dramatically revealed in Jesus' Calvary experience of finding a Resurrection of life and love (his Father) in his very worldly, earthly dying. There was Someone worth dying for. And so, a cruelly absurd death is rendered beautiful to us and encouraging for our own life and death in this world, in what it reveals of a fullness and presence of life and love that is, in a sense, beyond any experience here and now, but yet which is finally available to all of us in Jesus, our Father's kept promise of intimate hope.

But how do we experience, before death, the Father of Jesus in his transcendence beyond this world? For some, it is available in the dramatic, peak experience of crisis, when choice is both forced—and offered—between the consolation of a God greater than this world's absurdity and—nothing. Either—or. In the critical moment when all of this world seems absurd and inimical, loving surrender to a God greater than all of this and whose love conquers all averts ultimate despair and destruction. People led through this experience learn to root their faith more deeply in God than ever before. Born again, they learn to see the world very seriously, and as much more valuable and precious than ever before, because it is the stuff of a beloved Father's Kingdom.

Not all are called to, or allowed, such a crisis. But this fundamental and essential experience of God is not available only through crisis. It is, at base, a contemplative experience, a conversion experience, of God which is available to every believer. Nevertheless, as Paul describes in *Romans* 6/1-11, and whether it occurs in a resounding crisis or in a quiet, secret, outwardly ordinary transformation, it does involve sharing Jesus' death to this world—in order to live for God. There *is* a choice. And we do make it, whether suddenly or over time. Either God, or the world. In being attracted to the choice of God above the world, one then, of course, can find and live with God, and for God, within the world.[6] And then, the apostle is in sight: the one who, having chosen God and not the world, is now available to be called by God, sent by God, to serve the world, *God's* world—the world God loved so much he sent his only Son.

Through this experience, then, whether critically peak or not, but genuinely assimilated, we learn neither to take the world too seriously nor to take it lightly, either. A heart stretched by such an experience of God is simply not susceptible to an involvement in this world such that this world seems to be its own and our ultimate meaning and justification. For this is secularism pure and simple: no God, really; but if acknowledged at all, a God locked into this world. Jesus in all his serious concern for this world was never involved as though it were all he had. His identity center was never in this world, but in his Father: in his dear Father, whose love was greater than life itself.[7] This was what kept Jesus energetically free in his life in this world, for this world. And so, too, for any disciple of Jesus.

This experience of God beyond this world, which is meant to identify all of us in Baptism, also prevents a seriously un-Christian making light of this world. An excessive dichotomy between heaven and earth can lead people to long for the former and tend almost to view this earth as valueless, or, at best, as a dangerous distraction. Such a lack of serious concern for this world can never result from an authentic experience of Jesus' Father, but only from a failure to appreciate another aspect of Jesus' Calvary experience—his own embodiment of his Father's love and care for us sinners in this, however sinful, immensely beautiful and precious world. Jesus is not someone irresponsibly unconcerned with this world, but neither is he someone so in love with this world that his freedom and ultimate identity are limited to it. Rather, his center is always a dear Father who is a source of all his worldly love and life.

This special religious experience, of having our identity in a God beyond the world while being actively involved in it, is no once-in-a-lifetime experience. It is rather a lifetime process renewing, deepening, remembering and repeating our God-in-Christ experience. We must recognize the means God sends into our lives to renew this central, identifying experience. We must also find regular (daily?) habits that assist to renew this central focus of our heart's vision. Together with many service situations each day, liturgy, a healthy practice of mortification, and formal prayer can be regular reminders of a Father whose love and care for all of us point far beyond the transitory world to a fullness of Spirit still gifting a dying Son's trust. The final beauty for us and for our world—God himself—not only shatters any narrow secularism, but invests our proper apostolic concern and action in the world with a paschal force which labors joyfully that everything may belong to Christ, who shall hand all things over to the Father, that God may be all in all.[8]

Against this background of a strong, secularizing tendency in our world today, I will now treat a number of other trends and issues on the American spiritual scene. Some of these concerns are more directly affected than others by our secularizing world. But all of them, in my judgment, are susceptible to its influence.

III. RELATED TRENDS AND ISSUES

1. A Sacred-Secular Split. A division of our world into sacred and secular is one of the chief tendencies of secularization. Father Philip Murnion recently told the Catholic Theological Society of

America that "we are experiencing (a) disaffection from faith and Church and a separation of private Church life from public social life that is the main feature of secularization."[9] Many call for a political theology which would heal this split and bring the Gospel more to bear on the persons and institutions of our unjust, sinful world. Such a view rightly understands that to theologize and to practice spirituality without a passionate concern for the specifics of our world only exacerbates the sacred-secular split and that the approach is, in any event, unchristian. But conversely, any merely external activity, however much on behalf of justice, is equally insufficient to heal this split wherever it exists, whether within an individual person or within a community. Any attempt at healing which neglects the split at the level of *interior* experience risks a fragile solution that will quickly slip into an unrooted, social externalism. Evangelization must aim deeply *and* broadly: it must essay healing the split deep within the individual human heart even as it confronts the systemic injustice in our society. Liberation theology needs to be rooted in a liberation spirituality for the individual believer.[10] The silence and solitude, the healing purification and conversion of the encounter with God cannot be bypassed. Segundo Galilea articulates it exactly:

> Authentic Christian contemplation, passing through the desert, transforms contemplatives into prophets and heroes of commitment and militants into mystics. Christianity achieves the synthesis of the politician and the mystic, the militant and the contemplative, and abolishes the false antithesis between

the religious-contemplatives and the militantly committed.[11]

The ability to deal in faith with a wide range of inner affective experiences in our hearts makes possible finding God in every inner experience. In this way all human experience gradually becomes religious experience and culminates somehow in God, thus healing the split between experiences which are either overtly religious or secular. Without this inner integration in faith of a person's on-going experience, political theology and spirituality are both unrooted—just as the inner faith integration, if left to itself and without the outer word and action, becomes unreal and, finally, impossible. A careful discernment of heart expressed in a passionate concern for individual evangelical issues and in a courageous loving presence to the serious social issues of our world will avoid any unjust, unfaithful, secularistic dichotomy.

2. Global, Societal Values. As we look to the future, there is an urgent summons to transcend overly personalistic—or, perhaps better, individualistic values. In the midst of a growing, democratic stress on the value of each human person, Vatican II took as one of its central foci the value of the person. In the last chapter, while affirming this value as utterly central to the Christian mystery, I nevertheless treated the danger to personalism of a subtle self-centeredness. And I suggested we might be ready for a more refined Christian personalism.[12] As we look forward now to the year 2000, when global and societal problems will be, even more than today, an inescapable reality, our education and religious formation must be founded on global, on societal, values rather than on simply personalistic ones. Learning to cooperate, throughout both national and international society, will become, will have to become, more and more the truest meaning of personal fulfillment. And questions such as these will face us if we take such a global perspective: How do we take account of the millions of poor starving people in our world as we arbitrate labor disputes for excessively high salaries, whether we are talking of air-controllers or of baseball players? How do we overcome the natural tendency to get as much as one can for oneself, rather than to think of sharing with millions upon millions who have much less?

We have a long way to go in this shift of value perspective before the year 2000. The heavily personalistic approach (really, it is better to say individualistic) with its selfish stress on self-fulfillment, will not convert and develop easily to a global perspective. The conversion involved here will be a whole new way of thinking. But it must go beyond that—to a change of heart. This global view will finally be shaped in experiences, carefully planned and reflected upon, as a complement to serious study. True Christian personalism, of course, which is not narrowly individualistic, has no need to renounce any of itself, but will find a ready ally and field for service in global, societal concerns. Indeed, Christian personalism will become fully itself only in a communal, universal perspective which incarnates that justice, love and peace which mark the Kingdom of Jesus' Father.

For most of us, the shift we speak of calls for a change of heart that must run deep, get radical and become a revolution in our sensibility.

3. *Unity and Diversity.* On April 8, 1979, at an academic convocation in Cambridge, MA, Karl Rahner, attempting a theological interpretation of Vatican II, claimed that this Council "is . . . the Church's first official self-actualization as a world Church."[13] And Rahner claims that as the Church takes this revelation of her global nature ever more seriously, there will necessarily develop a pluralism of proclamations of the one Good News for many new cultures in Asia, Africa, and other places. How shall we find a true unity of faith within such a pluralism—and without again reducing it to a Western, Roman, overly centralized uniformity? Philip Murnion, in commenting on the unmet challenges of Vatican II, feels that: "It is now the *basic* ecclesiology of Vatican II that confronts us as we grow weary and dissatisfied with so many superficial expressions of this ecclesiology."[14]

As this basic ecclesiology of a "world Church" begins to be realized in practice, the pluralism which we know already can only radically increase. And as we are very well aware, such rapidly growing diversification often brings in its wake confounding disorientation, high-strung tension, and even hostile, angry charges of disloyalty. The problem is, and will be: *faith*—to seek, and to learn to recognize, *unity of faith* within diversity. That said, however, we cannot simply float with an almost infinite variety, as though diversity, in and of itself, were pure value. Finally, *both* human intelligibility and Christian faith require a unity. But a unity underneath and within diversity is not always easy to perceive, especially when diversification is rapid and recent. In a time of great diversity, before a clear, profound and pervasive unity has been found, we must learn to live both honestly and charitably, and with inevitable tensions.

But even as we are patient, we must also continue to search for, we must ambition and work for, that unity which will help us understand how diversity is a blessing, how it enriches and does not enervate. Simply to settle for a tolerance of plurality is not healthy pluralism. Whether it be a matter of the forms of ministry or orders, or of women priests, of religious garb, of doctrinal expression, or of forms of Church membership, we must continue to grow toward a "coherent consensus that can serve as a basis for common and confident Catholic identity."[15] As we search for a deeper coherence and discerningly reflect on much experimentation, we must reverence one another and the intricacies of ecclesial authority and development. And the best way we reverence both one another and the issues is by sharing our beliefs as best we can, from deep within our hearts, in the confident hope that a God who is so joyously one precisely in terms of his own lovely diversity will guide us together and will help us to see the extent and limit of diversity—so that we may be one even as Father, Son, and Spirit are one.[16]

When looked at institutionally, the area of ministry may especially seem to reveal a diversifying revolution that verges on the chaotic.[17] We speak of "ministry" now, where before we would have said "apostolate" or, simply, "work." Many believers, especially those professionally trained, now speak of having a ministry. This explosion of ministries has unhooked the word, and permanently so, I should think, from a past, unambiguous relationship to ordination. Now, in word also, as always before in fact, it is not only priests who minister. And this great multiplication of ministries through the 1970's is no mere matter of a word. It signals an underlying ideological shift regarding ministry in the Church.[18] Various studies are trying to expose this ideological shift, so that it may be clear to all what it may mean for the future, then discussed and carefully experimented with, before any long-term decisions are made. This development in ministry is very complicated and needs to be studied from many perspectives. Perhaps serious consideration of the renewed ecclesiology of Vatican II will help us appreciate the theological source for much of the development regarding ministry in the Church. For if the Church is seriously perceived as mystery and not just as institution, as community and not only, or even primarily, as hierarchy, as mission and not just as haven of the saved, then much of the ministerial multiplication becomes not only intelligible, but rich and welcome.[19] Hopefully, then, such study will gradually expose the underlying issue here, so that we can choose our future in a diversity expressive of a profound, commonly shared faith-unity, rather than be trapped in a future diversity which is only the bitter sign of the disunity of unconcerned or warring parties.

4. *Spiritual Witness of Religious Life.* Part of the explanation of the great expansion of ministries is the urgent sense of the countless challenges with which the modern world confronts the Church. There are so many opportunities, and there is so much to be done.

And we have not the leisure to wait; time is running out.

This urgent sense of ministerial opportunity and challenge is affecting religious congregations in at least two different ways. Some groups, over the past few years, have learned the futility of furious and relentless activity and are now involved in a serious, mature, realistic program of spiritual renewal. And they are doing this without any unrealistic or self-centered withdrawal from apostolic activity. But rather than trying to do as much as they "can," members are taking means and time to improve the prayerful *quality* of their presence and action in the world. Some leisure, to keep personal spirituality and humanity alive, is not seen as time wasted or selfishly spent, but is encouraged to provide the spiritual, faith motivation requisite for a courageously loving and enlightened presence in the critical situations of our world.

There are other religious congregations that would almost certainly not explicitly deny the necessity of serious spirituality to root serious ministry. But at the *operative* level, they at least seem so taken up with their difficult ministeries that fatigue, often verging on burnout, prevents serious growth in prayer and in the inner resources for that personal love relationship with God which alone can motivate authentic apostolic service. In such congregations, often there is not much specific encouragement from superiors and other leaders for prayer, for careful spiritual reflection, or for time taken for serious retreats alone with God. Members of these congregations sometimes look in vain for such encouragement, and they wonder at an apparent lack of appreciation for on-going spiritual renewal. These groups are frequently grappling with the crucial issues of our age, and often with great courage. But they are also doing so, often, with an apparent lack of any realistic, informed and detailed concern for that inner life of the Spirit which keeps apostolic life prayerfully focused on Jesus' revelation of the Kingdom of his Father.

Within the significant, contemporary trend of religious congregations moving—not theoretically, but operatively—in two different directions, the issue is the subtle integration of the inner and outer, of prayer and ministry. I certainly have no wish or competence to sit in judgment on who attains this integration and who does not. Either of these two directions I have described can be exaggerated. Excessive care of spiritual practices can produce a "hot-house" pietism unconcerned with major issues in our world. And excessively busy activity in our secular world, without sufficient spiritual resources—and taking the time for this—can burn out faith and a prayerful spirit, in a way that does not further the Kingdom. As we confront the fact that ministry is not a matter of staying as busy as possible, we can be led to the deeper, more subtle issue of a careful concern for the *quality* of our action—a quality determined by the graced availability of our hearts and wills to God in all we do. We will struggle with the fluctuating mixture in our consciousness of grace and sinfulness, of consolation and desolation, and see how seriously related it all is to our service. An active apostolic spirituality, never a matter of simple busy activity, is as much a matter of this inner quality of heart expressed in a special human, faith presence, as it is a matter of courageous activity and service for God's people. As this is more appreciated, the groups now moving in the two directions I've sketched above will not judge or belittle one another. No, they will incresingly cooperate in diverse ministries, through a shared and prayerful faith.

A related trend here concerns the role and understanding of *formal* prayer in serious spiritual growth and in mature ministry. Obviously, mature ministry is impossible without mature prayer. Here, I do not simply equate formal prayer and mature prayer. By no means. The latter term stretches far beyond the practice of formal prayer, into a whole life of prayer—but only so, I suspect, because of an appropriately regular practice of formal contemplation. Without regular, formal contemplation, a mature, prayerful life in ministry does not seem possible. Most serious believers I consult and listen to, in the course of many travels and workshops, would readily agree with this. But many would then squirm a bit, perhaps, as they reflect on their own practice of formal prayer.

I sense some widely divergent understandings today of "regular formal prayer." Without wanting to suggest any uniformity for all, let me pose some questions that may help us candidly face the issues in this trend. To practice regular formal prayer, does a person need a specific, daily expectation of length and time, rather than leaving it simply to daily spontaneity? Does this daily expectation or ideal then leave one open to days when God "excuses" one for various reasons (his), thus preventing the ideal from becoming iron-clad and causing guilt? Is formal prayer always somehow a withdrawal from activity into the intimate solitude of our hearts to be with God there? Is praying formally once or twice a week what is usually meant by "regular," for a mature believer? Is it a different type and quality of prayer that one is capable of when one prays for thirty rather than ten minutes (without letting prayer become too clock-oriented, like a prayer-wheel)? Even in the case of quite advanced spiritual persons, is the disappearance of regular formal prayer, for at least 30 minutes, a bad, or at least, very questionable sign? I think individuals and whole religious communities must give serious thought to questions such as these before they too hastily agree again, even in very beautiful words, how important formal prayer is for busy apostolic lives.

I am not entirely sure what reaction these questions may call forth from various people. But I do sense a growing desire among religious and others to be more prayerful and to be more honest about the whole question of what it means to pray, and of the necessity of praying if one wishes to be prayerful. Many look for clear, specific guidance and encouragement in this matter. And this desire to grow in the practice of formal prayer, as a means to a life of prayer and service, is no monastic aberration for an active person. I sense we can be carefully more demanding of one another in this area, after a period of vague, rather general guidelines which reacted to some past inflexible, detailed programs of prayer.

How these questions about regular formal prayer can be answered by busy parents with small children at home must also be investigated. Though in general their spiritual ideal and program must be different from that of religious and priests, it is still not at all clear that they are incapable of some realistic, regular practice of formal prayer. Without proposing any seminary or convent style of spirituality for busy parents, we must not downplay either their desire for prayer, even at the cost of sacrifice, or the necessary interplay of protracted regular prayer and a developing life of prayer. But much more experimentation and study must be done on the adaptations appropriate to these people—but adaptations which will not trivialize the often significant spiritual capabilities and desires of these lay men and women.

5. Religious Life: Life in Community. Another trend seems also to be moving the understanding of relgious life in two quite different directions. Is religious life now, and will it continue to be, life lived in community? Once again, more operatively than theoretically, there seem to be congregations that respond yes to the question—though they may understand "living in community" in many different ways. And there are certainly congregations that—at least in the way they act—would clearly seem to be answering no to community life as a necessary element of religious life.

Some congregations see the profound unity of the whole group as springing essentially from that shared experience of "being sent" which integrates religious authority, obedience and mission into one life and call.[20] This profound sense of community in mission is then incarnated in each and every person's living somehow as a member of a local community, with exceptions occurring only because of the necessities of geography or the nature of the particular ministry. In this way there is a clear incarnation of the belief that a member's heart is given over completely to God and his people, but it is given to God and it is given apostolically precisely through belonging fully to this specific congregation. In this understanding, apostolic community is not an end in itself, but it certainly is a continually essential means to ministry and service and thus is an essential aspect both of religious identity and of apostolic action.

In other congregations, life in community seems experienced and desired and chosen as much less essential and pervasive in the group. And these groups are often composed of competently trained, talented, generous people. But their apostolic service seems more an individual concern. They are often found either living alone or, when they live together, they seem to do so more as a matter of convenience and/or compatibility than as anything required to express their identity. They often live the vows seriously and carefully, though where ministry is not an experience of "being sent," there would seem to be difficult questions about genuine religious obedience.[21] Operatively, whatever the theoretical aspects may be, there seems to be a different view of religious life here—something more akin to what we have traditionally understood a secular institute to be.

The issue, it seems to me, is whether these two, clearly differing developments are also contradictory and therefore unable to be seen as authentic variants of one reality: religious life as understood and lived in the Church. Will we continue to see religious life as life in community—which has seemed to be one of its essentials since Pachomius organized eastern monasticism? It is important not to see community here as simply a geographical, local matter. That is an important meaning, but it is not the first nor is it the essential meaning of religious community life. Rather, vowed community life is fundamentally a profound union and *communion in mission,* a sense of the *corporate,* which indeed ordinarily is incarnated in a shared local setting of life and faith. Even now there can be tension and friction between groups of these two very different understandings of religious commitment. And I am not sure that the issue would not become serious enough in the future to cause a break and division in our understanding of religious life.

A major superior recently told me that she expected, after the relative peace and the low number of departures during the end of the 70's, that the early 80's would bring more upheaval and departures—but all leading to something deep and good, something more gospel-based. So there may be radical purification again! And a sizable part of this upheaval may well concern the precisely *communal* dimension of our lives as religious. People may leave either because of a desire for more shared life and faith than a particular group has to offer, *or* conversely, they may leave because of a loss of aptitude or affection for celibate religious living after years of individualistic living and working.

In congregations committed to a healthy, contemporary sense of communal living, there is another issue developing: a growing need for leadership on the local level. Groups, in and of themselves, still seem to find it very difficult to make decisions. Rather, they often haggle over each side of a question and often cannot move ahead. Beyond the role of a provincial superior and counselor, a local leader seems needed, a leader who listens, who values the communal and the collegial, but one able also compassionately to confront and to call individual members to be honest and prayerfully discerning about their lives, ministries and vocations. Leaders, then, are needed who are willing to accept the burden and service of authority. Without the encouragement of such a leader of the scene, honest, prayerful discernment about serious issues frequently does not happen. Provincials know how often they are confronted with the *fait accompli* in serious vocational decisions that have had very little consultation and prayerful discernment behind them. Mature, competent, professional adults, overly involved in our secular world, often need this careful but honest dialogue, if they are to stay in touch with, and live out, their deepest, truest desires in faith. But as provincials know, it is very difficult to find men and women of this leadership caliber, men and women both suited and willing to be facilitators and leaders of local community life. And of course there remains in some members authoritarian hang-overs which militate against this move toward better community living.

Another angle of this issue concerns younger members' entering religious life. Because of the serious decrease of members in the past decade, there is generally a real age gap developing between members who are about ten years professed and novices or temporary professed, who now face the prospect of joining for life. Can such young persons live and serve with members decidedly older than themselves? Can they live without much peer support? This is an issue which, in its detail and developments and implications, is quite different from anything most of us had to face years ago as we entered religious life. Today, the decision for final profession, for such young religious, will require a strong sense of vocation indeed, a sense of vocation that is rooted in a special inner psychic strength and a quite different type of trust in God than was asked for in the past. This sense of vocation and commitment must, finally, be rooted deeply in the inner solitude of the individual heart, where God's call continues to resonate deeply and very lovingly. Now the motivation must run *palpably* deeper than any horizontal peer support. The community dimension of our vocation, important as it is, can never replace the uniqueness of a vocation rooted in the experience of solitude alone with God in one's heart. In many ways, today we are being called back to this rooting of a religious vocation in *God*—in and through, of course, but also far beyond the personal fulfillment of shared support and affirmation. As *Ps.* 73 says of him: "You are . . . the future that waits for me."[22]

All these different aspects of this trend concerning community and religious life finally issue forth with decided impact on the level of felt membership. Today, unless one is a major superior or has been chosen for some other special responsibility in the congregation, the felt sense of belonging may grow dim. So many religious today, whether it be their own responsibility or that of others, feel disconnected, left out. In past times, there were so many details, such as dress, daily schedule, interaction with local superiors, shared fun on vacation; all of this specified the commitment and gave a person a living sense of membership. But many of these experiences are gone now, and so the sense of membership of the rank and file can get hazy, unspecified—perhaps, even, unreal.

This undefined sense of membership will haunt us, and it will be one of the causes leading to departures as we enter the 80's. Somehow, our sense of membership must newly and more intensely involve a sharing of vision, life, mission and faith, according to the charism of the whole group. But it must also involve careful communication across all levels of the group, and, finally, and maybe most importantly, it must seriously attend to the spiritual and human dynamics that work in the local living scene—and within the province as community, too. Ultimately, though, and deeply connected with this chapter's major theme of secularizing tendencies, the matter, while entirely human, must also be seen as entirely about mystery and faith. Faith must be very strong, if the practical, daily effects of faith are to have and retain their power to support fidelity, to sustain a *life* choice of God in the limited, definite way of life which is *this* particular religious congregation.

6. Distress Over Poverty. There is a growing distress and uneasiness about religious poverty in many congregations. It ranges from a paralyzing guilt to a vague uncertainty. And few other matters can so easily occasion anger among members of religious groups. Congregations whose ideal of religious poverty is clearly understood and is often very central to their identity may well not share this distress. Although I am treating this trend here in terms of religious life, in various ways it affects many other people in the Church. Frankly (and far from all will

will share this view) I don't think the precise issue has developed clearly enough yet within the ecclesial community. But I do think that the distress involved is a grace and that it is a stubborn, repeated call from God to rely more on him and to live in solidarity with all our brothers and sisters. If that's on the mark at all, then of course it would be a serious mistake to reject out of hand this uneasiness, however much we may like to treat even our healthy guilt in this fashion. There surely is some unhealthy guilt involved, too. But a good part of our distress comes, I believe, as an invitation from the Father of Jesus to take his love more seriously, especially in our excessively consumer-oriented American society.

So we must learn to live calmly and carefully with this annoying concern, until we come to know what in it is of the grace of God, and how we are to respond. In the meantime, of course, we cannot just sit and wait—often the worst thing to do with guilt. Rather, we must take whatever steps, large or small, are clear. Careful experimentation, both individual and communal, must be undertaken, together with prayerful discernment of our fears and continuing study of the significance of religious poverty in each congregation's charism.

In a world where billions are equally trapped, whether in the evil of economic poverty or in the parallel evil of excessive consumerism, a religiously motivated poverty must be carefully, not narrowly, understood. How do we find today a viable, contemporary apostolic significance for what has been one aspect of the tradition of religious poverty, that "all things are held in common?" In congregations where poverty was clearly an important element in the forming of the original founding community, how do we renew that aspect of poverty for apostolic community today? How do we all—lay persons, bishops, priests, religious—take seriously Jesus' invitation to a radical gospel poverty?

I hope our energy for this issue will not fritter away in excessive anxiety, but will rather generate a more radical discipleship of Jesus, a greater bondedness with one another, and a service that more reveals Jesus' single-mindedness in furthering his Father's Reign of love in human hearts—hearts learning to trust one another and him, in childlike simplicity.

7. Family: Development or Destruction. The state of the family in our culture continues to be cause for serious alarm. I spoke of this trend in Chapter Two and will add only a few brief comments here.[23] As people reflect on the summer 1980 White House Conference on the Family, with its organized sessions across the country, many feel overwhelmed by the enormous variety of understandings of the family, a variety clearly springing from a confusion of values held or spurned by various participants. Indeed, there was such lack of agreement on basic values that not only was it impossible to make any headway in discussing specific problems of the family, but even a satisfactory description of what a family is, in relation to marriage, sexuality and children, proved impossible. An excessive, secularistic tolerance for pluralism seemed to dominate discussion. Though there were some helpful conclusions and recommendations, the Conference did not really grapple with the issue of the values clearly involved in this trend of family development.

We surely cannot narrowly stick to any past understanding of family which rules out growth or development. Alvin Toffler, author of *Future Shock* and, more recently, *The Third Wave,* claims that "only some seven percent of Americans still live in classical nuclear families. The nuclear family is simply no longer the norm—and it is not likely to become the norm again, no matter how much pulpit-pounding or breast-beating we do about it."[24] As new forms of family multiply at a dizzying rate in our country, it will take great care and a deep sense of Christian moral values to sort through this rapid and very secularistic development, in order to choose new forms that are consonant with our Christian beliefs. It will take great care—and great counter-cultural courage.[25]

8. Women's Rights in Church Leadership. The previous chapter concluded with brief, very tentative comments about sexist language in referring to God. That trend continues with us. But it is even clearer now that the issue runs as deep as the honest acknowledgment of the fundamental human equality of women with men in Church membership and leadership. The issue, of course, is taking its most public and currently tense expression in the women's ordination question.

The possibility of the ordination of women continues to be researched, discussed and dealt with in some of its many aspects. From December 1979 through July 1980, three dialogues were held by representatives of the Women's Ordination Conference and the U.S. National Conference of Catholic Bishops. Their purpose was "to discover, understand and promote the full potential of woman as person in the life of the Church.''[26] Many of the difficult questions connected with the issue were seriously investigated, and the sessions concluded with an interim report. Some interested scholars now conclude that "there already exists something approaching theological consensus that there are no intrinsic obstacles to the ordination of women; the pastoral need for it is evident; it seems probable that it would be acceptable in those parts of the Church which are asking for it."[27] Still others would claim that much more than theology is involved: "Theologians must finally decide the properly theological aspects of the women's ordination question. But in so doing, they need all the help they can get: from biology, sociology, psychology, and the other sciences, yes; from the biblical renewal, yes. But also, from philosophers. For first of all, we need to know who we are, and what our sexuality is, and how we come to know what we know."[28]

There is also, inevitably, a real spiritual dimension to this issue. Without Roman permission, some women in this country have apparently taken the matter into their own hands.[29] Other women feel so put down, so victimized, that they cannot share Eucharist, while others cannot share active membership in the Roman Catholic Church at all. In certain situations, some priests feel beleaguered and fear to preside at celebration of the Eucharist, much less to concelebrate one, when women are present. And they are anxiously careful never to broach the topic in public conversation.

I can only renew my own hope, in this difficult time, as the issue remains with us and as it develops, that we may all be able—as mentioned in Chapter One—to grow in a sensitivity to correct past injustices in our own relationships; to beg for light in the Spirit regarding what *is* growth in this issue for the future; and to pray to live and serve generously in the present situation, with the humility and the urgent patience of Jesus in his passion.[30] Like all great events in human and ecclesial life, the question of women in the Church, including the question of women's ordination, is not simply a question or problem. It is also deeply mysterious. And to the extent that it is a great question, it will partake greatly in Jesus' own paschal adventure, his life-giving meeting, through suffering and death, with his Father. Jesus spoke forthrightly and boldly against injustice and oppression and in behalf of his Father's little ones. But he was also liberator, and never more powerfully so, than when he suffered and was taken advantage of.

9. Lay Colleagueship. Institutions that have a religious relationship, e.g., universities, high schools, hospitals, orphanages, and so forth are feeling pressure from many angles. The number of religious working in these institutions has severely decreased. And it requires great sophistication, at best, to secure the federal or state funding needed to keep such works going, and yet have any hope of maintaining an explicit religious orientation. People will usually go to a public institution, where the cost is less, unless the religious institution has something especially unique and valuable to offer. So, pressures threaten the very survival of these institutions, and more and more of them will fail to pass the survival test.

Ideally, the unique values that institutions have to offer must be rooted in the vision of the religious congregation to which the institution in question is related. If this vision is to take effect, however, there must be large-scale cooperation between the religious group, usually very few in number, and the large cadre of lay workers. Without the support of these lay colleagues, the institution will not even survive, much less have a specific, religious vision and spirit. More than just working *for* religious, lay persons must be seen as working *with* them. And if the special vision of the religious congregation is to be real and attractive to others, it must be thoroughly understood, believed in, and shared by the competent lay persons who help form the major part of the staff.

Many of our lay colleagues are eager to share our vision and to let it energize their lives and their work. But in most instances, there is a long way to go in this matter of lay colleagueship. Do religious believe in their own vision? And can they articulate it for purposes of concrete living and working, and in a way that is attractive to colleagues? How do we help lay colleagues develop spiritually in a way that is appropriate to them? Without violating affirmative action programs, how do we use our vision, after specifying it in goals and objectives and programs, in the hiring process?

Underlying this trend, of course, is the enormously serious issue of lay responsibility in the life of the Church. How much real responsibility is the Church willing to give to lay persons on all levels? Some people feel that "it is becoming increasingly necessary to articulate the place of the lay person in the life and ministry of the Church."[31] They wonder:

"Is it necessary to become clerical or religious to enjoy true responsibility in the life of the Church?"[32] The Church in many ways has yet fully to answer this question. She will only do so clearly, one way or another, not mainly by words but by the way she treats lay persons. A serious lay colleagueship, absolutely essential for the survival of religiously related institutions, hangs in the balance.

10. Seminary Training and Preparation for Priesthood. In the previous two chapters, I have treated the spirituality of diocesan priests.[33] And in conclusion here, I want to touch again on a few aspects of this issue, especially as it relates to seminary training.

My experience this past year suggests a growing concern for spiritual formation programs in diocesan seminaries. What should be the elements of a serious spiritual formation program in a diocesan seminary—one that does not treat seminarians either as monks or as active religious, but one which also does not tolerate a spiritual seriousness any less ambitious than that proposed for monastic and active religious? At least one diocese this year will try a "novitiate" period of intensive spiritual formation. Just as we have academic norms for ordination, how do we develop norms for requisite development, prior to ordination, in matters such as mature prayer, prayerful apostolic zeal, and affective, spiritual maturity? How do we come to that kind of shared vision and seriousness about spiritual formation which will engage the cooperation and collaboration of both academic professors and spiritual directors on seminary staffs? After facilitating a workshop last June for the National Federation of Spiritual Directors (NFSD) in diocesan seminaries, I am a bit more optimistic that the problem is being faced in some seminaries across the country.

Though this spiritual issue is certainly the most serious one, there are other important concerns affecting diocesan seminaries. Celibacy is one. Priesthood in the western Church at this time is very clearly a celibate affair. However, when there is such a dearth of priests, how seriously do spiritual directors in seminaries investigate a student's vocation for evidence of a clear, healthy call to celibacy—and in such a way that a genuine call to celibacy becomes a clear norm for entrance into theology and for approval for ordination? The severity in the world-wide shortage of priests continues to increase, leaving many persons and groups throughout the world without the ordinary sacramental ministry of the Church.[34] This shortage simply cannot be turned around quickly. It is doubtful that it will be turned around at all. It is a shortage that cries out for a reinterpretation of some of the issues touched upon in this article, e.g., ministry diversification, women's ordination, lay responsibility. But this severe shortage can also very understandably create an excessive, distorting concern over the need for numbers, on the part of bishops and seminary rectors, and it can foster naive hopes, on the part of prospective priests, who wish to respond to such a severe pastoral need.[35]

Seminary training these days is surely not easy. A humble confidence is needed on the part of both staff and student, a confidence and trust that can only come from growing spiritual maturity and an expertise that helps us to understand the dynamics of spiritual development and helps, also, to root a priestly vocation deeply and surely in the solitude that must be the center of a celibate heart—a heart that relies trustingly and ever more thoroughly on a loving Father, as the heart of Jesus most surely did.

Chapter Four

1983: A God For a Dark Journey

This year's survey of spiritual trends and issues is, fundamentally, simply a continuation of the last chapter's perspective and approach. That is, it directly assumes and builds upon the extensive description of secularization—rapid, continuing secularization—as the major influence and context within which all American spiritual life is being lived. I remain persuaded that, from many different angles, there continues to be a concern and struggle in American spirituality both to balance on the tightrope of the secularization of contemporary faith life and, at the same time, to avoid the easy missteps that lead, whether gradually or abruptly, into secularism.

All the trends and issues of this chapter, then, whether explicitly or implicitly, relate to the basic theme: our spiritual struggle as American Christians to incarnate the life and love of God in our rapidly secularizing world.

1. The God of Darkness and Suffering. Our rapidly secularizing and highly technologized world can be very deceptive and misleading. In most of the world there is, or at least can be, light of whatever color and intensity all through the day and night. No more darkness. Computers, cameras and cassette radios and recorders seem to promise constant companionship and communication. No more isolation. And yet, together with all this garish light and constant talk, there is a lingering and growing sense of darkness, alienation, poverty and loneliness. For a while we could read of three wars in the papers each day: in the Falklands, in Iraq, and in Lebanon. Though the inevitable destruction and carnage of those wars was disguised and quieted temporarily, gradually the terrible details are revealed. Slowly but stubbornly the economy squeezes not only comfort and convenience, but hope and life out of many jobless poor in this country. Most of the world events and concerns mentioned in the last chapter continue to be active among us.[1] This suffering and violence often visits a despairing darkness and emptiness upon the human soul.

To find God in this darkness and emptiness is a growing challenge. Because, for most of us, God is more obviously associated with light, fullness, wholeness, and with the beautiful richness of being, people today have more of a sense of forsakenness and abandonment in the empty darkness. The immediate future of our secular world will not bring a sudden evaporation of this darkness and alienation. Rather than attempting to escape the darkness, therefore, we must learn to look deeper into it, to find a God present everywhere—and always a God of personal love and intimate care.

The negative, or apophatic, element in the experience of God, then, may be taking on more practical importance today in spirituality. As Brother David Rast has said: Only if we can know a God whose transcendent greatness allows him to be no-where, can we gradually experience our God as always now-here. It is the approach of Pseudo-Dionysius and *The Cloud of Unknowing,* which leads beyond the superificial light of God's love into the depths of a darkness of faith where the God of love and light is experienced in a great simplicity of presence and faith. The experience needed here is the one I described in the previous chapter[2] as the protection against secularism. Now I think we are facing some specific implications of this experience of God.

If we do not settle for a God who is too small, then we can find a God of light, fullness, wholeness and beauty in the pervasive darkness, emptiness, fragmentation and horror of our world and our hearts. A God whose greatness and majesty can make human hearts tremble in awesome wonder is also so inextricably involved in all this world that the intimacy of love in Jesus can quiet human hearts even in the most fearsome and trying situations. As events in our world and in our personal lives shock and strip us to the very core of our being, we must, rather than despairing and falling into an unreal world either of denial or of naive optimism, learn to plumb the depths to find the God who holds all being and each of us in existence. In the depths of a heart experiencing pitch darkness or crass evil or chilling emptiness, there is present a God without whom being and existence cannot be. And this God, our God, is always love. It is the God whose love and care was always present to Jesus on Calvary, even when he sensed a chilling absence.

We are now struggling, and we will continue to struggle, to find what Louis Dupré calls *The Deeper Life.*[3] We need to discover the God whose pervasive and intimate love is finally revealed more fully through the negations of an apophatic spirituality, but whose love, like a quiet flame at the center of all being, is sometimes like a torch for great zeal and at other times like a white heat apparently consuming while actually laying bare the divine center of our true identity. Dupré describes the attitude involved in this profound experience of God: "Unconditional trust without knowing what it is we trust, willingness to let go without knowing whether anyone will ever catch us, preparedness to wait without knowing whether we will be met. Total looseness and unconditional trust are the virtues negative theology teaches us to cultivate. There could be no more appropriate lesson in our time."[4]

2. *The Temple of the Human Heart.* In a rapidly secularizing world, public life provides less and less of the genuinely religious. Shrines and temples seem useless. The decay of their buildings speaks of a dead past. Christendom has long since died and is not even a desirable ideal any more. The world and society are no longer built or structured according to a Christian vision, nor according to any genuinely religious vision. For many people this seems no great loss. But for the person of faith and religious sensitivity, the situation presents a great challenge.

Realizing the futility of turning back contemporary developments and trying to return to a past age's public religious expression, we are being invited to enter the temple of our own hearts. It is not enough that the ontology of every human heart makes it actually a temple of God. We need consciously to appreciate this and to cooperate with the adornment of this uniquely personal temple. Without a sense of this personal religious temple, faith can die as the heart falls prey to secularism.

This temple of the human heart cannot be wholly an inward reality. It must find some appropriate externalization. This inner sanctuary, of course, must be highly personal and intimately religious—a profound meeting of God and our truest self. And yet, while profoundly personal and intimately unique, this inner temple should not promote an individualistic privatism. The human heart where God lives and is adored and loved cannot become a church unto itself. The God who is known and reverenced in our own hearts is the source of, and the invitation to, community: the community both of the human family and of the Church. This religious temple of the heart, if its air is to remain healthy and invigorating, will require, especially in a secularistic, religionless world, some appropriate external aids, like a designated chapel in a religious community, or a special place in one's room, and a special time set aside for regular prayer.

But when the human heart has become a carefully provisioned temple of the Lord, a person becomes capable of an inner life of quiet intimacy and peace everywhere, whether it be in a bustling subway, or in the solitary confinement of a jail, or in the dangerous crowding of a refugee-boat or on the death bed of a cancer patient. At times our hearts will be temples of bright light focusing on a God joyfully imaged and named in Jesus. At other, catastrophic and confusing times, this temple will be darkened and will house a God temporarily nameless and unknown. In either atmosphere, this temple is a place where we bend low in quiet awe and reverently trustful abandonment to a love that fires ministry for God's justice in our world.

This profound inner life of personal religious experience will be increasingly necessary as we move to the future. And it is always available, because of that God whom Jesus spoke of as seeing and rewarding all hidden gestures of love: " . . . Let it be a secret between you and your Father. And your Father who knows all secrets will reward you."[5] Karl Rahner, in an article on "The Spirituality of the Church of the Future," sums up this trend and its issue for the future: "It has already been pointed out that the Christian of the future will be a mystic or he will not exist at all. If by mysticism we mean . . . a genuine experience of God emerging from the very heart of our existence, this statement is very true and its truth and importance will become still clearer in the spirituality of the future."[6]

3. To Be People of the Church. Many people continue to grapple with the role of the Church in their Christian identity. Whether it be intelligent, gifted novices in a religious congregation or serious students in a seminary or spiritually serious students in college or young people returned from some special volunteer service after college and on the verge now of entering a parish, the issue is always the same: in living a genuine and generous love for God, how much must one be a person of the Church? And the issue centers on the institutional Church. Can I stand for and identify myself (maybe in some necessarily special way) with this international institution of the Catholic Church? For some it is a matter of conscience, whether they have to identify with some of the practices and policies of the Church. Many, while believing in God and living generous lives of service, either explicitly reject membership in the Church or operationally live their religion without any real relationship to the Church.

This is a complicated matter but one that must be faced by the whole spectrum of Church membership, from Pope and bishop to parishioners in the pews. A specific cause, or combination of different causes, can raise the issue for various people: a domineering clerical attitude; monotonous, uninformed preaching; a successful remarriage after divorce; the prohibition of women's ordination—or maybe even the prohibition of their service as lectors; and many other reasons. For an increasing number of people, practices within the institutional Church which they perceive to be unjust are making membership in the Church more and more painful and questionable. To questions about how much one must identify with the institutional Church, answers would range far and wide. Some would almost identify the Church with the institution, while others would play down the institution to almost no significance—and some would even think the question otiose.

A sense of Church must be reclaimed for many people. For the fully Christian mind and heart, the mystery of God in Christ Jesus, and therefore the mystery of the whole human family, is incarnational and communal—and universal. All this says community. And not just sect, either—but Church. But it must be a Church that is attractive, inspiring, demanding, inviting. The development of such a Church that others can believe in will continue to be the task of all of us. The Church on all levels of membership must continue to struggle for a more genuine following of Jesus in our world. Some gather regularly into small groups to share life and faith and find support in community. This can begin to provide an experience of community, which is at the core of Church. But it does not, in the long run, suffice. To see the glory of God in a weak, human Church struggling in the Spirit—this is never easy. It requires a stubborn hope, the hope of a genuine lover, sometimes surely a critical lover, but always a lover of the Church.[7]

4. An Expansive Ministry Born in Forgiveness. Especially in religious life, but also throughout the whole Church, it is getting more and more difficult to find people competent and willing to undertake ministries of difficult responsibility. In religious life some major superiors speak of a crisis of leadership. They speak of a lack of available and suitable men and women for challenging roles of leadership either in the religious community itself or in the apostolic works of the community. It may be a formation director, the pastor of a new black or Hispanic parish, a third world mission assignment or a superior in a larger community. But the issue is always the same: men and women to fulfill these challenging tasks. We have renewed our concept of the role-model for a religious superior and for the leader of our apostolic works. But it is difficult to find men and women suitable and willing to undertake such missions.

Paramount among consequences of this leadership crisis is the interference it is causing with the service that religious communities could otherwise render in the world. This leadership need is not to maintain past outmoded structures, but rather to inspire and facilitate more unified and effective service in response to new, serious challenges facing the Church in today's world.

Is this leadership failure a result of faulty formation? This is a question worthy of reflection on the part of all of us. And it must be answered carefully. The profound renewal of contemporary religious formation has involved a necessary development in a direction quite different from the past. The stress on individual responsibility and careful respect for the gifts and talents of the individual has correctly tailored formation programs increasingly to the strengths and weaknesses of each individual. But while moving in this person-oriented direction, we have not, perhaps, maintained or developed as well as we might have that healthy sense of self-abnegation which would allow an individual to be truly available for more of the service-needs of the religious group. This is a necessary correction/refinement of contemporary formation that we now recognize and can implement. In an earlier chapter, I called this the development of a more refined Christian personalism which would help us recognize and transform the very real, though subtle, self-serving tendencies in all our hearts.[8]

As we ponder the difficult ministries facing us now and in the future, we must remember that all genuine ministry is rooted in devotion. Ministry is neither something carelessly superimposed from above, nor something narrowly limited to an individual's comfort and convenience. Devotion here is not some emotional pietism. Rather, it is the experiential capacity to find God—something that runs much deeper than emotion and feeling. Formation programs should provide a great diversity of experiences, in order to stretch the person's capacity for devotion far beyond what might have been originally expected. If an individual's ability to find God is too narrowly limited, that person's lack of availability for service can easily become a future liability.

This trained experiential ability to find God in various ministries and situations always involved a self-transcendence. This is a transcendence made possible through an abnegation of self which is motivated and inspired by an experience of the greatness of God's love for me. The goodness of God's love is exhilarating and expansive, and attracts the human heart beyond narrowly self-centered concerns. Heroism for God is born here. But without a growing mortification, which is not destructive but revelatory of our true self in God, the devotion of finding the expansive joy of God's love in many future ministries simply is not possible.

Another aspect of this crisis of leadership for ministry is our ebbing experience of forgiveness. Forgiveness is meant to be the birthplace of great zeal for ministry. God's gratuitous forigveness sets off a dynamic which extroverts a heart for service. To be forgiven beyond one's wildest dream is not something to be kept to oneself, but becomes a life of service to others. The greater the sense of forgiveness, the greater and more expansive will be the zeal of devotion for finding God in ministry.

But a trend already mentioned continues to haunt us in this whole matter of a vigorous availability for ministry which is essentially rooted in the religious experience of forgiveness.[9] And it is this: We remain timid and confused in our admission of personal sin. As we continue to grow out of an unhealthy, Jansenistic, legalistic sense of sin (especially in the sexual realm), we are left with a vacuum since we have not yet properly assimilated a healthy sense of social sin or of personal sin (also in the sexual realm). Fears of self-hatred and unhealthy guilt still dull our sensitivity to the healthy guilt and shame that is always part of the grace of a forgiving God seeking out the sinner. But so long as our past leaves us confused and quite unresponsive to our present sinfulness, we cannot experience the full dynamic of God's forgiveness in our hearts. And it is only an acknowledged sinner, humbled in the truth of forgiveness, who receives from God an expansive zeal for ministry.

The effect of a shallow experience of forgiveness finally registers in ministry. If one is not driven to ministry through forgiveness, one can fabricate one's own ministry in too selfish a manner. Rather than receiving a ministry from God in the devotion of forgiveness, a person can cling to a ministry with an angry arrogance and impatience that often speaks of proving and aggrandizing oneself, rather than serving the needs of others. Further, this experience of being humbled in the truth of one's sin and God's forgiveness is always an important sign distinguishing a true prophet from a false prophet. In these days when prophecy is a more noticed phenomenon among us than before, and when we are in need of the inspiration of true prophets, we cannot forget that the true prophet is forged in the zeal and humility of forgiveness.

5. A New Way of "Making" Catholics. Any remedy for the deficient sense of personal sinfulness mentioned in the previous trend will require much more than our renewed rite for the reception of the sacrament of reconciliation. This renewed rite, in practice now for about eight years, though it is an improvement, has obviously not by itself renewed many people's experience of God's forgiveness. What is needed is a whole catechesis to help people recognize in their own hearts the dynamic of receiving God's gift of forgiveness.

This raises the issue of how Catholics are formed and trained, raised in the faith these days. It is a matter of how people over a life-time continue to enter the Church. There seems to be a great change occurring here which will have tremendous implications for the future. Most of us were raised in a Catholic school system where we had drilled into us the essentials and practices of Catholic life. But things have changed. There are not nearly so many religious serving as teachers as before. Many parish schools have closed. And besides, many of those simple, clear essentials of a Catholic life are not so simple and clear any more.

As formal Catholic schooling becomes less and less available, CCD and other methods of religious education take on greater importance. Often in the past CCD was not very effective. It was perceived as a definite second-best to the parochial school. But that view is slowly changing. And it must continue to change. As the whole structure, procedure and atmosphere of formal schooling becomes less and less the chief way to hand on faith, some new replacements must be instituted. Genuine Catholic believers will never sprout fully grown from the ground. Besides learning the doctrines of faith, young people must receive a feel for the faith life. They must be allowed to admire it as they see it lived and shared by others. As Michael Warren, an expert in youth ministry claims: Young persons need the fidelity of adults who care for them.[10]

The Rite of Christian Initiation of Adults has received good press. Some have called it "a revolutionary document" as it ritualizes a process of initiation into the Church which "gives first priority to the mystery of God's love for us."[11] It can also be used as a guide in the baptism of infants.[12] But while this document expresses a better view of Church and ritualizes much better the process of initiation into the Church, its effectiveness will very much depend on the proper attitudes of priests and laity and the availability of enough competent, generous, committed adults. Only in this way will the words of the document come to life as a real on-going process of initiation, a real catechumenate, which can help transform both how we "make" Catholics and what genuine Catholic life will look like in the future.

RCIA, then, over a period of years, can play a large role in the formation of Catholics, but it cannot dispense us from the serious experimentation needed to discover and develop forms of religious education that will be effective through the young years and on into adulthood.

I do not want to be misunderstood. I am not calling for the abolition of all Catholic schools. I am, rather, speaking of the realistic situation facing us now. The cost of private religious education continues to escalate as we struggle to arrange tuition tax credits to cover some of the expense. And, as mentioned earlier, the number of parochial and private schools continues to decrease. In this situation, we must find a viable replacement for handing on Catholic faith and helping young people to grow up in that faith. Both in the schools that remain and in new religious education programs, the role of competent, enthusiastic lay people continues to grow in importance. And this brings us to our next trend.

   6. The Growing Vocation of the Lay Person. We need to broaden our understanding and usage of the word "vocation." One often hears the worried question: "Do you think we'll have enough vocations?" The question clearly limits the concern to priestly and religious vocations. In breaking out of this past narrow understanding, we need to help others to see that living a serious faith life involves for everyone a vocation to service in the Church. It is not only priests and religious who have a vocation. Even a lay vocation can be viewed too narrowly, as Archbishop Bernardin has cautioned: "Sometimes the impression is given that if a lay person wishes to become involved in the Church's mission, he or she must always be specially trained to become, in effect, a kind of professional within the Church. This view of lay ministry, I believe, is too narrow."[13]

   As a broader sense of vocation develops and spreads, I think we will never know exactly how many vocations (in the narrower sense) are "enough." But we will cooperate much more in all sorts of Christian ministries—and so we will feel much less shorthanded. Attitudinal changes, however, among some clergy especially, and among some lay people, too, are needed before that older limited view of vocation is transformed into greater collaboration on all levels of the Church.

Both the need for, and the supply of, well educated, committed lay men and women continue to grow. More and more lay men and women are needed both to share and implement the religious vision that must shape the curriculum of our parochial and private Catholic schools and to exercise other ministries in parishes and dioceses. A growing number of competent people are available for all these posts. And increasingly they are men and women hungry for an adult, inspiring and integrating spirituality. If these people are not to search for this spirituality outside the Church, we must provide ways to respond to this hunger. And this assistance must be largely centered in the parish. In no way does this exclude the use of special spiritual centers or retreat houses or programs outside the boundaries of the parish. But these must always be complemented by a lived sense, within the parish, of spiritual growth and challenge—growth and challenge manifested in things like the quality of homilies, small discussion groups and a strongly collaborative response to the missionary needs both within and beyond the parish. Dolores Leckey, executive director of the U.S. bishops' Secretariat for the Laity, lists as primary among the needs of the laity: "a place to tell the truth, the experience of being listened to with respect, a chance to minister in ecclesial or designated ministry, and affirmation of the secular lay vocation and support of that vocation through theological education and in-depth spiritual formation." She sees these needs calling forth three needed attitudes in the ordained priest: commitment and community, interdependence in ministry, and willingness as opposed to willfulness.[14]

For many of these lay men and women, the vocation to which they are called is the noble and glorious one of raising a good, happy Christian family. I have reflected earlier in this book on the present precarious state of the family and the challenges with which this situation confronts us.[15] Without repeating some of those points again, my concern here is simply to face and restate the need for holy, self-sacrificing men and women to give themselves to raising a family. In a culture tending more to self-centered comfort and convenience, this ideal of raising a family tends to lose some of its glow. In fact, how many young people, once they finally settle on marrying, plan on having a family? It is hard, though, to know how pervasive this attitudinal shift away from raising a family really is.

The vocation of a mother and father, with its own unique suffering and sacrifice, must never seem "ordinary." It is a great, glorious vocation, and one vitally essential to the future of the Church and the human race. Talented and dedicated young men and women must be helped to see that raising a family is truly a vocation in the Church. A theology and spirituality of the family must continue to be developed for the contemporary world and Church. Only with continuing reflection and careful cooperation on the part of husband and wife can their raising of a family become integrated with, and be a powerful, creative means for furthering, their own profession and sense of self-worth. And the legitimate, essential struggle for women's rights must not be allowed to create a condescending scorn for the woman whose life for a number of years is spent at home raising a family. To co-create with God, and daily to reveal God's love to children, is an exalted vocation—one that gives profound joy and binds parents in deeper love, through all the sacrifice.

7. *Public Witness To a Gospel Spirituality Undercutting All Political Ideology.* The Church has been taking more and more stands on social questions over the past three years. A quick review of the issues of *Origins* would show how often the National Conference of Catholic Bishops has spoken out and testified before various Congressional Committees over this same period. Some names of Church men and women have almost become household items on various social issues, in this country and beyond. Nuclear disarmament, international human rights, aid to El Salvador, an anti-abortion amendment and the abolition of the death penalty are but a few of the issues that have drawn public stands from various bodies within the Church. I would guess that, as the Church's social consciousness continues to grow, there will be need in the future for even more public stands.

There is a serious danger of something that could corrupt the Church's whole approach to social issues in this country and throughout the world. Some of the courageous stands that the Church is taking and will be called upon to take may well coincide with stands of different political ideologies, whether Marxist or capitalist, Democratic or Republican. But the Church's stands must always clearly be articulated and justified as—they must both be and be seen to be—conclusions of a gospel spirituality which undercuts any and all political ideologies. One can, these days, hear someone speak strongly for international human rights or nuclear disarmament, or for any other social issue, but who does so in such a way as to become clearly involved with a specific political ideology. When people hear such a talk, they often, and quite reasonably, wonder how a speaker of other political views would address the same topic. When a speaker's viewpoints are given in such a partisan manner, any gospel vision, if expressed at all, simply has to lose much of its force. And so the gospel witness is blunted for the hearers. A specific political orientation of a speaker, therefore, can often distract from the power of a position sincerely intended to incarnate gospel spirituality. To be identified too closely with a political ideology, rather then to be and act as a person of the Gospel, distracts people from what can be the power of various public, social stands of the Church. To be ready to take such stands requires that the individuals involved in these issues continue to take means to grow in and live more profoundly a gospel spirituality.

In its first version of the pastoral letter on peace and war the National Conference of Catholic Bishops claimed that "war, especially the threat of nuclear war, may well be the central problem of our age." Within the past two years much energy and effort has resulted in a gradual development of sensitivity and consensus, not only on the part of the bishops but also, though more slowly and perhaps less perceptibly, on the part of the Catholic faithful. How extensive this consensus will become and whether it will prevent a serious division among the faithful at the publication of the final version of the pastoral letter this Spring is hard to predict. But the different titles of the first two versions of the pastoral letter do manifest, for the present, some of this development. "God's Hope in a Time of Fear" becomes "The Challenge of Peace: God's Promise and our Response." Some commentators have seen the first version as inviting Catholic theologians to develop a true theology of peace and the second version, in response to an avalanche of helpful criticism, as an actual contribution to such a theology. Joseph O'Hare's words seem very sound and sensible: "In the end, the process may prove more important than the document it produces."[16] The dialogue, debate and honest confrontation of different positions, at times quite heated, seems a work of the Spirit painfully forming a clarity and consensus that can challenge not only the consciences of Catholics but also the difficult decisions of those responsible for the peace policies of our country.

This complicated issue of the use and even possession of nuclear weapons must be both carefully scrutinized and evaluated, finally, in terms of an explicitly gospel vision of reality. The bishops must speak, and must be seen to speak, from a different vision than those simply working within "liberal" or "conservative," or "left" or "right" ideologies or categories. The seriousness of the issue, which may be honestly summarized as the very survival of the human, deserves the most careful searching out and testing of consensus within the American Catholic community. It must be a consensus based upon our richest moral consciousness. To settle for any minimal, lowest-common-denominator would be to default on the great spiritual leadership incumbent on the bishops as leaders of our faith community.

In many different ways we can be instructed by this process. It can teach the bishops and the rest of us about appropriate ways of reading and facilitating the Spirit's formation of a faith consensus within our community. It can instruct us about what shall have to go into the future meaning of an internationally accountable, authentic patriotism. It can help us learn experientially about the essentially important matter of unity and division within the American Catholic Church in the face of a great public issue which is profoundly moral and intensely political.

Religion, and not just moral perspectives, shall have to be part of what we are taught. A profound and comprehensive peace, which God's love as revealed in a crucified Son can bring to human hearts, is what alone makes possible genuine conversion and love within the whole human family. This peace of God is the heart of the matter. And Jesus is God's victorious promise of this peace.

Besides this crucial issue of peace and war, there are other aspects of our concern for justice to be mentioned here. As we continue to increase our concern for justice, there can be a tendency to become too narrow in vision and even to exaggerate the justice issue—even though it very rightly continues to grow in importance. And again, lest I be misunderstood here, let me reassert that I do realize how very far many of us have to go in developing a true sense of justice and letting it influence the dedication of our Christian lives.[17]

However, as can happen with almost any issue, we can so stress an orthopraxis that our concern is chiefly with immediate activity for social justice rather than with developing a vision that can enlighten and invigorate all the works of the Church, and not simply the social works. For example, in the work of a professional in higher education, besides direct social service when possible, there are many other means for inculcating in students attitudes for service and long-range social change. Professors who do not manipulate or dominate, but who serve their students by staying alive to their subject, who keep their classes well prepared and challenging, are very directly promoting justice. A view suggesting direct social service as the best if not the only way that higher education can serve God's justice in this world seems a far too narrow, and therefore false, position on what is involved in the integral promotion of justice.

A similar exaggeration of the justice issue can overlook the spirituality needed to give force to any social concern. Though most of us still have a long way to go in sensitizing our hearts to God's call for justice, I wonder whether, for some who have decidedly moved the center of gravity of their own involvement, the challenge now is to find and maintain a viable spirituality within the new central thrust of their lives. A flurry of social work is not enough. Christian commitment to the works of justice must spring from a profound sense of God's love always at work and most dramatically promised in Jesus' Calvary experience of dying into a fullness of life and love. Among religious, an extreme tendency can yield

to the temptation of settling for what Johannes Metz
has called the political dimension of each of the vows,
without a struggle on the part of the religious to integrate the mystical with the political dimension so as
to develop an organic life of concerned service.[18]

The struggle for justice can also become un-
focused and lose its gospel foundation if it forgets the
mutual interaction between those internal, individual,
more personal dimensions and the external, social
dimensions in our human world. This struggle for
justice must always involve the careful balance and
interplay of the evangelization of individual hearts
and the formation of a just world society. Concerns
about stealing, cheating, abortion and sexual im-
morality must always be carefully related to concerns
of international human rights, nuclear disarmament,
politics and economic justice. Some individuals, some
religious communities and other Church groups who
are laboring nationally and internationally for justice
and liberation, must be careful lest they seem caught
up in liberal causes of the day which claim to pursue a
systemic, social justice without enough concern for
the conversion and sanctification of individual hearts.
A just society will always require more than a political
and economic system. The justice and liberation we
are concerned with here is of God. It is God's sanctification and liberation of human hearts in Jesus.[19]
But this is a liberation that can only be incarnated in
our world through humanly cooperative analysis,
planning and action. The sense and grace of its being
God's work through us can never become empty
theory, but must always throb in the veins of an apostle for justice. Liberation theology must always be

131

energized by a spirituality of liberation.[20]

This difficulty of keeping the individual and the social, the internal and the external in proper balance runs deep in the modern mind. The issue is too comprehensive to be treated here and will surely not be changed overnight. But it needs urgent, serious attention. In a world overly interpreted by scientism there is, of course, little or nothing beyond the physical. Metaphysics has fallen on tough times. What you see is not only what you get, but it is all there is, in this modern view. This development of modernity has a long philosophical foundation beginning in the sixteenth century and developing through the Enlightenment. It is an issue of huge proportions, far beyond any possibility of more than mention here. But it should not surprise that this issue insinuates its way into our struggle today to understand and to integrate that justice without which faith is incomplete, that justice which demands not only social action but moral conversion of soul.

8. Bridge-builders. Besides a growing need for prophets in the Church today, there is an equally great need for bridge-builders. The pioneering prophet always calls and leads a people into the future. The builder of bridges is needed to keep the body of the people together and not let them be separated. In many areas polarization is not as severe, or at least it is not so obvious as it used to be. But on all levels of the Church there is need to bring people from different viewpoints together in a genuine unity beneath and in and through their differences.

The work of the bridge-builder is creative, patient, and very difficult. It is creativity that prevents community from capitulating to the least common denominator. In the face of certain impasses the ingenuity of an engineering feat is called for to bridge the gulf. Bridge-building is also messy work: you have to be willing to get dirty. To dive underwater and survey the depths, to lay foundations in muddy ground and to set steel and cement is never easy. It is very patient work, work that stretches a person. One must be able to live on both shores, to recognize the gulf of difference and to have a genuine desire and hope for bridging that gulf of difference. The builder of bridges learns to listen compassionately, though not uncritically, to the good of both sides and doesn't become trapped on only one side. Bishop Cummins of Oakland, when talking about the changing relations between bishops and theologians, called his brother bishops to "be wise enough to consult not just those theologians with whom we are intellectually comfortable, but even a wider group so that we will have the sense of the broader reflection and experience of the community."[21]

Bridge-building is a priestly work in imitation of Jesus who is the great high priest, the *Pontifex* (which in Latin means a bridge-maker). It is a priestly work we can all practice. Just as Jesus' priestly bridge-building is best revealed in his salvific suffering and dying on Calvary, so our own bridge-building ministry will involve a passion of patient suffering which will always be creative for unity. Today, we all need to develop some of this creative, paschal charism of bridge-building, if we are not to settle, on all levels of the world and the Church, for a shallow, easily disrupted communion of minds and hearts.

133

9. On-going Monastic Renewal. In Chapter One, while surveying the decade of the 70's, I mentioned the matter of renewal in monasticism.[22] During this past year, the issue has been brought home to me again with some intensity. Some members of monastic communities obviously feel it is time for some honest, thorough evaluation of all the experimentation of the last fifteen years. They sense that communities are too easily presuming the validity of too much of that experimentation.

Though this issue is somewhat removed from my own personal experience, I am sensing in certain voices, not just a traditionalist tendency, but a healthy call for evaluation before monastic communities move on much further with planning for the future. In the midst of the much healthy development which recent experimentation has brought, are there some changes that have weakened rather than strengthened the monastic experience of God in the Church? How, for example, do the sisters of a renewed contemplative community resolve their growing wonder about whether they have lost too much silence in their life together? How does a monastic community recognize and reject the newer versions of a tendency to rigidity, legalism, boredom, self-satisfied complacency—signs always antithetical to the Gospel?[23] These questions, and there are many others that monastic communities could formulate far better than I, are not easy questions. But they could provoke stimulating, life-giving evaluation.

In the long history of monasticism, it has been a complicated matter to determine the appropriate "works" of a community. Merton has reminded the monastic community that it "does not exist for the sake of any apostolic or educational work, even as a secondary end. The works of the monk are not justified by their external results but only by their relevance to his monastic life alone with God."[24] Louis Dupré, in a powerful chapter on "The Poverty of God," while commenting on the monastic lifestyle, says that "the monk avoids looking ridiculous by refusing to take himself or his work more seriously than they deserve. Measuring them against the backdrop of eternity he rightly judges human concerns to be less than all-significant."[25] The traditional "work" of hospitality continues to bring many people into touch with the powerful monastic witness and source of faith in God. Perhaps it can be an extension of hospitality today to be involved in explicitly spiritual ministries, such as direction, or other temporary services rendered to the local civic community—often done right in the monastery. Of course the details of such determinations can only be known in the light of prayerfully careful study of the spirit and writings of the founder or foundress. And by planned, scheduled evaluation.

It will always be a challenge for the members themselves to believe in the monastic apostolic style of *being* and to resist any inappropriately active style of *doing*. We speak here of more than a rearranging of schedule or works. It is a matter of renewing an attitude and a vocation of men and women called to witness to God, our eternally faithful Lover—called to do this through who they are and how they live together, rather than through what they "do" and "accomplish."

As some monastic communities try to evaluate the developments of recent years, they may be helped by re-reading Thomas Merton's "Memorandum on Monastic Renewal"[26] and by looking at Louis Dupré's conferences to the monks at Gethsemane,[27] and a host of other writings on the monastic life today. And if, as some are suggesting, this issue requires further attention, perhaps the Association of Contemplative Sisters in this country could facilitate a prayerful evaluation. Monastic life is at the very heart of Christian faith and justice. In a secularistic world so hyperactive and quick to identify and evaluate people according to what they do and have, the joyful witness of men and women whose basic identity is to *be* in apostolic contemplation before God, while always difficult to maintain, becomes ever more important.

10. Developments in Religious Life. New religious groups continue to appear in the Church. One meets new religious communities that have broken off from an older, better-known congregation. Some impasse could not be resolved and a new group was born. There are other new groups that are not offshoots of any previous congregation. Some of these groups have canonical and ecclesiastical approval; others do not—and some are not interested in such approval.

There is much vigor, value, variety and novelty in all of this. All these groups are responding to some need but often in quite different ways. Some are permanently formed groups, founded in the permanent covenant of final profession. Others are bound together much more temporarily. It is important to acknowledge the valuable service rendered by all these groups, when they are not dominated by an ugly reaction to a past difficult situation.

Can all these groups be classified as religious life? Are there new forms of religious life appearing in all of this? How far can the traditional understanding of religious life be stretched in new directions? It is still too early for this observer to be sure about any answers to these issues.

My personal conviction is that we must be careful that religious life cannot come to mean almost anything. Otherwise words lose meaning. It would seem clear that the Spirit is breathing new types of groups into the Church at this time. And it is not necessary to force all of them into the framework of religious life. I myself incline to think that religious life will continue to be a life of total consecration to God, specified in terms of celibacy, poverty and obedience, lived in community,[28] and with explicit ecclesiastical approval. In light of this understanding, though there can be much renewal of forms of religious life, there probably are not any wholly new forms. But there are, and will continue to be, new forms of communities that are not formally part of religious life. And this, rather than being a problem, should be a welcome addition to ways of serving in the Church. To be mutually understanding and to serve together in building that Kingdom of Jesus' Father in human hearts, as it grew and was revealed in Jesus' own heart—this is the most important gift to receive from God and to share with each other until time and experience give us greater clarity about this issue.[29]

Another development in religious life, and for various reasons a cause of sadness and discouragement for some, is the continuing departure of men and women both before and after final profession. As I mentioned in the last chapter,[30] evidence seems to support the belief that the number of departures which decreased in the end of the seventies is now picking up again in the eighties. Such a phenomenom needs to be pondered. It can contain a call to keep renewing the lived witness of religious life. But, it seems to me, here we have a phenomenon different from the sixties and early seventies. People realize more and more what the truth and demands are of a religious vocation in the world today. The immediate reason for many people's leaving seems to be related to celibacy. For them, celibacy does not seem right and good, if possible at all. But to settle for this as a final, adequate explanation seems usually too simple. Investigation and reflection upon so many of these cases reveal, for instance, that observance of religious poverty has stopped and at least the attitude, if not the execution, of religious obedience of mission has also weakened or even stopped before celibacy also lost its gift quality and began to seem a burden too heavy to bear any more. Though celibacy may be the more immediate and obvious final issue, it cannot be separated from religious poverty and obedience, both of which buttress and give expression to that interpersonal, unique companionship with God which, at its core, is what celibacy is all about.

11. Openness to New Non-Western Ways of Seeing Reality. Over this past year, missionaries have brought to my attention this final trend. As the Church continues to grow in Africa, Japan, India, and other parts of the Near and Far East, the faith of our universal or "world" Church[31] can be enriched by openness to the very different ways of perceiving reality in these countries. But it will require a flexibility that is not always easy for us. My own limited experience and reading in this area prevents me now from writing about the obviously vast and important implications of this openness for our Christian future. But I sufficiently feel the truth of the witness of these missionaries to want at least to mention the matter here, at the end of this chapter—with the hope that both reader and writer will ponder this further.

Chapter Five

1984: ASSESSING AND CHOOSING
EVEN AS THE JOURNEY CONTINUES

The exhilarating wind of Vatican II, by means of which the Holy Spirit breathed and even gusted through the Church and world, introduced a period of special experimentation and very challenging transition. This final chapter in what has been a collection of annual reflections and commentary, over the last five years, on the contemporary American spiritual scene, is very much influenced and focused by a sense of a special, quite specific stage we have come to in this post-Vatican II transition. It seems to me that from many points of view we are being called to assess and take stock of our pilgrim journey since Vatican II—without, of course, closing the door on further development. We remain, and very rightly so, very much in the midst of a period of transition in the Church. But within that transition, I believe we are now also in an extended moment that asks for a careful and honest evaluation of what has been happening, with a view to appreciating where we stand at this point and what we have learned thus far. Stocktaking time, therefore,—assessing and choosing—even as the journey continues.

This chapter, then, begins with a brief description of this special moment in our corporate pilgrimage. After that I will treat some trends and issues which seem to me part of this special moment of assessment and accountability, whether influencing it, influenced by it, or both.

I. ASSESSMENT IN THE MIDST OF TRANSITION

Both experimentation and evaluation always play important roles in the healthy development of any human organization. One without the other is always dangerous and, finally, destructive. To be carefully and constantly evaluating life, but without experimenting with it much, is to stagnate and to make evaluation otiose. On the other hand, frequent experimentation and change that is not regularly focused and disciplined by some serious, discerning evaluation quickly misleads. It can be exciting at times, but finally it will violate and even destroy a basic identity. And all this is so both of persons and of groups.

As the period of special experimentation mandated by *Ecclesiae Sanctae* comes to a close, we are witnessing various efforts at review and evaluation. A prolonged and elaborate study of American seminaries is presently under way. A document on "Essential Elements in the Church's Teaching on Religious Life as Applied to Institutes Dedicated to Works of the Apostolate" has been published by the Sacred Congregation for Religious and Secular Institutes[1] to help the American bishops "to encourage and strengthen religious life in its authentic renewal."[2] Furthermore, a new canon law for the Church has been promulgated. And many religious congregations are involved in getting their constitutions approved by the Holy See. These are just a few signs of the special phase of evaluative reflection now taking place in the Church.

How this process of evaluation is interpreted and how it will be carried out is of the very greatest importance because, while the official period of special experimentation mandated by the Council may be terminating, the Church itself continues to be involved in a profound, extraordinary transition and development. We are still passing through one of the few critical upheavals and periods of radical change that the Church has known in her long existence. And whatever some might wish, there is no sign we shall be done with it any time soon. Very fundamental realities, like grace, faith, sin, mortal sin, the sacraments, and so forth continue to be conceived and articulated in very new ways. The moment of careful evaluation I am describing here is not meant to bring this extraordinary transition to a halt. Therefore, the evaluation and accountability due will not be written on stone—for it is not a time for setting norms and essential elements in any rigid and finally settled way so as to prevent future development. Nor is this evaluation in any way a matter of "getting back to the way it used to be" before all the change and turmoil. The moment of assessment and choosing I seek to describe here marks no such narrowly 'conservative' move or victory.

In any time of extensive, vigorous transition, it is important both to maintain a sense of identity rooted in tradition and a profound on-going, actual experience of God's love and care actively inviting a trusting surrender in the Spirit. These are the essentials of genuine development in the midst of rapid and rampant change: It takes both a sense of identity in the tradition and a profound experience of God to give the discerning insight necessary for careful evaluation and for decisive choices. But when grounded in this way, a decisively honest reflection and evaluation can confidently sort out, momentarily, true and false developments and can point the direction for the continuing growth of God's people as led by the Spirit of a God whose fidelity, promised in Jesus, will never, finally, contradict the tradition but will rather develop, stretch and bring new life from that tradition, at times in exciting and even shocking changes not fully appreciated in the moment. In this connection we must remember that the knowledge and love of history, the history of the Church, of spirituality, of religious life, is as important as is our hope in the future. For history teaches vividly—think of an instance like Francis of Assisi—that the Spirit can do something so new and so apparently disruptive that only time and courage together with that deep peace of heart which allows patience will show it to be the Spirit of God building, and indeed building in a deep, mysterious, loving continuity with what that same Spirit has done before.

1. *Quiet Polarization Preventing Healthy Pluralism.* The vociferous polarization that so often occurred among us in the sixties and seventies has quieted down a good deal now, if it has not disappeared. It does not play to the gallery so often as it used to. But it is there. And most of us know that very well. Furthermore, I sense that this quiet, largely unspoken polarization among us often not only prevents a healthy, developing pluralism but often foments an unhealthy tolerance of mere plurality—that is, a polarization at those essential depths where we either are or are not a community,

are or are not fundamentally one in Catholic faith, are or are not one in Christ. And yet, as I have mentioned in an earlier chapter,[3] healthy pluralism will always involve, because it must involve, a unity of faith, clearly perceived and shared. Without such unity, rapid diversification can easily become tolerance of plurality—at times, perhaps, a plurality of beliefs of such moment and such depth that it defies unity and reconciliation. Such tolerance of plurality can be a lazy—or wary—settling for diversity without the hard work of that patient dialogue and honest investigation needed to develop, discover, and share profound unity in faith.

There are many examples today of positions quietly polarized beyond much, if any, dialogue. These polarized positions are not always clearly contradictory, but they often veer towards such collision. Two groups who view the Church in different ways—one in an overly juridical, institutional, authoritarian, "law and order" way, and the other in a more charismatic, pneumatic, participative way—often, and mostly quietly, go their separate ways. There are also profoundly divergent views about the relationship of faith and morality to sexuality. And, related to this issue of morality and sexuality, there are great ecclesiological differences, including understandings of what the magisterium is and what is its right to teach faith and morals for the faithful. There are some conflictual understandings of what religious life is, and, especially, of the role and exercise of religious authority and obedience. The understanding, significance and relationship of the priesthood of all the faithful and a special ministerial priesthood is another area where great diversity of view exists. The ordination of women and a married priesthood continue to be cause for deeply felt cleavage of opinion. The gospel of organized, systemic liberation for justice and the gospel of the conversion of individual hearts can tangle in conflict in a way that separates rather than unites.

Admittedly, these issues, used here just to exemplify the quiet polarization, are very complicated and rarely capable of easy solution. (Sometimes the solution does lie in seeing that one opinion is right and the other wrong. Very often, however, solutions lie in other, more integrated views of the particular matters in question.) My concern here is not to resolve and settle these conflicts. These situations, and many others, can be seen as examples of profound differences of opinion among us which often quietly polarize us. There is of course some but relatively little screaming, name-calling and public condemning related to these issues. But a clarity about the differences and a tenacity of conviction usually joined with a quiet, closed settledness, may be steadily dividing one opinion from its opposite. And so, underneath a surface unity of politeness and courtesy very often lie deeply divisive opinions that are rarely discussed. And it is this quiet, settled, accepted nature of the polarization that can be most dangerous.

At the heart of this phenomenon of quiet polarization we can usually find evidence of a too narrow and closed ideological type of thinking. This applies equally to conservative and to liberal views. A way of thinking locked into the narrow purview and comfortable assumptions of an ideology is very different from a way of thinking rooted in a profound

Gospel perspective and an on-going experience of God.[4] Of its nature such obedience to the Gospel and to any genuine experience of God is always open to being called away from a mistaken way of thinking to a deeper unity of faith. This is not to by-pass the facts that Gospel faith has an intellectual content, and that at times we must stand for an essential of faith against opposition. And it is certainly not to deny that minds professionally trained in philosophy and other secular disciplines are needed to analyze specific worldly issues. But it is to claim that a Gospel vision, besides the assistance of an educated mind reasoning carefully, requires a heart growing in the Spirit of Jesus as it is converted more and more from unbelief and a sinful self-centeredness.

We must learn to recognize in ourselves the signs of this tendency to get locked into a narrowly ideological way of thinking. One of these signs can often be a stronger desire for the victory of showing how right I am than a desire to be genuinely reverent in seeking and learning something right about another person's opinion. This tendency to a narrow, closed way of thinking is in us all and often goes undetected. But whether detected or not, ideology divides and polarizes. It forbids and erodes that dialogue which searches for a deeper unity of faith in Jesus within the diversity of a healthy pluralism.

Especially in this present moment of discerning evaluation leading to further transition and genuine development, this quiet polarization needs to be faced—and worked through. Honest and reverent dialogue about our differences brings enlightenment to everyone, a deeper unity of faith, and an increasing, healthy puralism. But to remain settled in polarization, however quietly, to settle for a lazy or wary tolerance of plurality, can only be an interference and, in my judgment, a grave one, to the tasks of this present moment in our pilgrimage together.

2. *A Phase in the Dynamic of Liberation.* Liberation, like maturity, is a terribly important process for every human being. Liberation *is* a process. So it never happens suddenly, but over a period of time, and it can be divided into various stages or phases. Liberation is also meant to be a growth to greater maturity. The process of liberation to greater maturity can be applied to an individual person, to a nation and to other groups of people, like blacks, gays, men, women. And basically it is the same process as applied in these different instances.

Though the process of liberation is meant finally to lead to healthy, mature identity, it usually, among other characteristics, involves a phase of rather exaggerated self-concern. This is a phase involving discovery of and fascination with the self, sometimes in strong reaction to a period of oppression and denial of self. This one phase—one of many involved in the process of maturing—is my concern here. It is not always a very balanced phase. But it is unavoidable. And since it affects not only persons and groups but liberation movements also, it therefore is going to affect how liberation movements have their impact on persons and on groups and on organizations, including religious congregations.

Because of the many different liberation movements currently at work in our world today, it is important that we learn to appreciate and deal with this one stage within the context of the whole process of liberation and maturity. The affirmation and discovery of self is an essential moment along the road to mature identity. But such preoccupation or fascination with the self, however necessary for a period, is not the goal of human existence. Love is. Human maturity is about self-sacrifice in a surrender of love. Nevertheless, it is precisely this affirmation and discovery of self which then makes possible the human maturity of surrender of self in love. Hence the essential goodness of this transitory stage in all liberation—because without this sense of self-possession, not always reflectively grasped and articulated, self-surrender in love, where possible at all, would lose much of its depth and energy and staying power.

A similar dynamic can be perceived in the development of a nation's identity. A nation's mature identity should involve it in playing its proper role in a careful balance of international relationships. But before this stage can happen, usually there is an excessively isolationist and/or aggressively nationalistic phase which pits this one nation against, rather than in healthy relationship with, other nations. There can be a belligerently superior and self-centered spirit to a nation while in this experience of excessive nationalism. For many countries this is a strong reaction to a period of oppression and domineering colonialism. Many third-world nations are struggling through this stage. Iran's ferocious anger in the American hostage-holding incident is perhaps an obvious example. We might wish that this excessively nationalistic phase could be by-passed on the way to a healthy international identity, but it would seem unavoidable. So we must learn to deal patiently with other nations as they pass through this early, understandable stage on the way to a more maturely integrated, international identity. We have other immaturities of our own as a nation seeking full maturity and liberation. Recognition of such limitations on our own part can provide motivation for patience with nations that may be involved in this particular moment of the dynamic of liberation.

This same dynamic of self-centeredness, finally, can be seen in the developmental process of various groups of people. Blacks, gays and women are some examples of groups involved in the liberation movement. In all three cases there can be no doubt about past unjust oppression and discrimination. And the predictable and understandable stage of excessive self-concern aimed at self-affirmation and discovery cannot be avoided. We can only unrealistically wish, therefore, that this stage will not happen in a particular liberation movement. Rather, we must learn to acknowledge this stage for what it is, in order to keep it in the context of the whole movement to greater maturity. In this way we can deal with it appropriately.

Since this stage is usually, understandably over-reactive and since it is certainly not a final stage of maturity, a liberation group—and any person, group of persons, organization, affected by a liberation movement—must be careful to avoid articulating its identity, or most aspects of its identity, from this limited, over-reactive perspective. This stage is a time suitable for tentative soundings, but not for judgments. While in the intensity of this over-reactive stage, neither blacks nor gays should fully define their role in society. Nor should women who are in a moment of significant influence from the women's movement. Nor should men who are in a moment of significant influence from the women's movement. And religious congregations of women, therefore, which might very understandably be moving through this reactive stage, must be careful, during such a period and from such a limited perspective, not to define in constitutions their own identity on essential questions such as the meaning and role of religious authority and obedience. (Of course, the point I am making presumes a continuing struggle and advocacy to convert the prejudicial attitudes of many men and women in areas where women are oppressed.)

A person or group in significant touch with Jesus and gospel values will deal with this temporary stage of understandable over-reaction to past oppression and discrimination in a way quite different from that of people whose lives are not so centered on the Gospel. They will manage their feelings differently as they pass through this stage. They may very likely even have different feelings. And they will act out this stage in a different way. But one thing seems sure: this is an unavoidable stage on the journey to greater maturity and, therefore, it will be neither prevented nor repressed by the Gospel.[5]

In this present moment of careful reflection and evaluation—this special time of assessing and choosing in the midst of transition—any failure to recognize and appreciate this temporary stage of excessive self-preoccupation in the dynamic of liberation could lead to serious misunderstanding and unjust evaluations which will damage authentic personal and group identity and will anger and divide rather than unite and open to further genuine growth.

3. Religious Life. I will treat in this section a number of trends that directly concern religious life. In the midst of the simply enormous amount of experiment and change characteristic of religious life since the Council two events are perhaps especially provoking the present moment of prayerful assessment for American religious: the issuance of the Vatican document on religious life to the American bishops and the effort of congregations to have their re-written constitutions approved by the Holy See. In some instances I will be reconsidering here trends which I have already examined in this book. Developments in myself or in the matters at hand have sometimes altered or deepened my perceptions and brought me to a greater clarity about possible issues involved.

a) A Public Witness to Christ and to the Church. The Vatican document makes it very clear that a public witness to Christ and to the Church distinguishes religious life from a secular institute. For the most part, this is a repetition, at this particular point in the history of religious life, of a longstanding view. And this publicly sanctioned witness in the Church determines many of the essential elements of religious life as presented in the Vatican document. The presence of religious life is "visible, affecting ways of acting, attire and style of life."[6] In line with this stress on public witness, it would seem that some religious congregations have unsuspectingly moved over the years closer to the classification that the document gives to a secular institute. Some interesting questions can surface at this point. How serviceable is this distinction now after many years of growing diversification and complexification in religious groups in the Church? Does this document express clearly and carefully enough all that we have learned about the distinction between monastic apostolic and active apostolic religious congregations—learned as a result of returning to the roots of our founding charism, as mandated by *Perfectae Caritatis* and as a result of our study of the development of religious life over the long history of Christian spirituality? Are some congregations meant now to develop into secular institutes? Will some congregations consider the option of extra-canonical status because of difficulty in getting revised constitutions approved or because of essential disagreements about religious life as presently described by the Holy See? Or will some congregations make further adaptations so as to reveal more clearly the public witness of religious life? How will some religious accomplish a needed reconciliation in order genuinely to have this relationship to the Church of a public witness? (I remember a sister commenting in a workshop on reconciliation that a fair number of religious are finding it hard to be reconciled to a Church that can be so oppressive, unjust and sinful in our world today.)

According to the Vatican document, public witness essentially involves life in a community in a "place of residence which is properly established by their institute in accordance with common law and their own constitutions."[7] In an earlier chapter[8] I noticed the operational divergence in religious congregations as regards whether life in community was seen to be essential to religious life. I think this divergence is still with us and must be reviewed in this time of evaluation. It is important to see that much more is intended here than getting every religious into a religious house. A corporate dimension in mission, faith, life and identity is seen to be essential to the public witness of religious life. This is a profound attitude of heart which must then take flesh and be explicitly incarnated in daily life. Again, some questions will be faced. How do we form specific local communities? How much of a role does the choice of the individuals involved play? What role does a religious congregation's missioning of the individual play in the choice of community? How do we justify an individual's living alone?

Another element of the public witness of religious life is the wearing of a "religious garb that distinguishes them as consecrated persons."[9] In another place the document states that "Religious should wear the religious garb of the institute, described in their proper law, as a sign of consecration and a witness of poverty."[10] Though it seems always a mistake to make this issue of attire and garb too central, this could be the most provocative statement of the Vatican document for American religious.[11] Some may respond by simply disregarding this directive. But I have heard a lot of concern, questions and discussion of the topic already. My hope is that the issue will not be exploded out of due proportion, but will lead to some serious experimentation with a religious garb that is publicly distinguishing, a sign of simplicity and poverty and in accord with the founding charism of the institute. Where the value of some special religious garb is accepted, still other intriguing questions arise which need further discussion, experimentation and review. Can a full religious habit (a word not used in the recent Vatican document but found in the new Code: canon 699, #1) be distinguished from a religious garb? And if so, does the meaning and purpose of a habit speak more to the charism of monasticism than to the charism of active apostolic religious life? Should the religious garb be basically uniform for all members? What role, if any, does a veil play as part of appropriate religious garb? What role does the culture of a certain country or of a local area play in determining appropriate religious garb? Is a religious garb something to be worn always or are there times when it is not necessary or is even inappropriate? Can a distinctive garb, at times, prevent the appropriate service intended by a religious?

b) Religious Authority and Obedience.

Recognizing authority and responding in appropriate obedience is always challenging for sinful human beings. Hence it is not strange that we still find confusion, fear and, at times, rebellious denial as responses to authority. This variety of response can be found among the general run of people in this country. Though there is a growing concern for "tough love" with its expectations and demands to be met, it is still quite true that an excessive egalitarianism and a narcissistic individualism have put the question in many people's minds and hearts, and on their faces: Who are you to tell me what to do?

Throughout the ranks of believers in the Church this same variety of response can be found. Whether it is papal teaching in morality or Vatican guidelines for religious life or the National Conference of Catholic Bishops' pastoral on peace and war,[12] the same question can surface: Who are you to tell me what to do? Oftentimes I sense among us religious that feelings bristle at the mere mention of religious authority and obedience. Much of our present reaction is due to a past overly authoritarian exercise of religious authority and a mistaken identification of immature, passive dependency with religious obedience. But a lot of the present difficulty may also be rooted in other forms of immaturity as well as in the perennial, common sinfulness of our human condition.

Perhaps some of this confusion about the existence, source and role of religious authority in religious life will be challenged by the recent Vatican document on the essential elements of religious life. Today there is not only diversity but conflict among the various views, experiments and practices in religious congregations regarding the functioning of religious authority. Sometimes this conflict seems to move toward irreconcilable positions. A number of people have mentioned to me that they found evidence of this sort of conflict about religious authority and obedience in some of the articles in the *New Catholic World's* very interesting issue on religious life.[13]

Some of this confusion and conflict will have to be addressed. Without intending either a lengthy treatment or a final resolution, I will list here some of the issues that seem to be involved.

1) Is religious authority invested in a specific person? The recent Vatican document speaks of religious authority "invested in superiors for the duration of their term of service at a general, intermediate or local level."[14] This religious authority is clearly conferred by the Church. When considering this directive, it is

155

important to distinguish religious authority from all other types of authority as well as from the charism of leadership—although in this latter case, while granting the essential distinction, it may be thought helpful to have religious authority conferred on persons who have a charism for leadership. The Vatican document is helpfully clear that religious authority, though it is invested in a specific person, is not to be exercised in isolation.[15] This invites further reflection and a discussion of the role of consultation and the role of participative, collegial structures of government which nevertheless acknowledge and facilitate the existence and exercise of personal religious authority. It is clear that a consultative, participatory style of government developed in recent years has brought many more individuals to a more active, adult sense of membership in their congregations. But further discussion will be needed to investigate and reconcile how members can both claim authority over their own lives[16] and relate appropriately to a specific religious superior.

2) How keep authority and government in an explicit context of faith? Sr. Mary Linscott sees our tendency to treat authority outside the context of faith as a real weakness in our effort to renew structures of authority.[17] She claims that "the reality of religious authority itself is not in question but that much of the crisis lies in the evolution of structures and the search for suitable styles of exercise.[18] In general this seems true. But in some cases I frankly wonder whether a confused understanding of the phrase "religious authority" does not disguise what really does amount to a denial of the existence of religious authority. Whether or not there are a few problems about the very existence of religious authority, it is clear that our greater concern and confusion now involves the faith perspective of authority and government in religious life. Some of us have so secularized our governmental terminology that the sound speaks to us more of business, managerial and political organization than of the profound theological and spiritual values of consecration in religious life. And the sound may be having far greater influence than we imagine. Our vocabulary and symbols have immense motive power, often subtle, even in areas where we may have little conscious intention that they do so. I have often been involved in discussions about the appropriateness of the term superior. Granted its obvious deficiencies, there is surely confusion and inaccuracy arising from some terms being used to replace it. Mary Linscott's reflection seems appropos: "It would be a great help to many if a more acceptable word were found. In the meantime we are caught between an unpopularity and an inaccuracy."[19] Fundamental, of course, in this whole question of considering the authority of a superior in the context of faith is our theology of Incarnation, our ecclesiology, our theology of sacrament. Do we believe in *mediation?* It is one of the most central intuitions of Catholic faith and an urgently important sign of Catholic sensibility. Do we share with our Catholic tradition the faith conviction that in some very serious, however corrected and purified sense, the superior stands and acts "in the person of Christ?"

3) Does religious authority derive from and reside in the members themselves? In my judgment, this is a live issue being debated by many. For some others it is an issue that has been settled either explicitly or implicitly, and perhaps in a way that would seem opposed to the Vatican document.[20] Some clarification here can promote valuable discussion and experimentation for future development. In the present understanding of religious authority as conferred by the Church on a specific person, it would seem that *religious* authority (as clearly distinguished from all other kinds) cannot be derived from, nor does it reside in, all the members. But it does leave open the question about these other kinds of authority that can reside in the members. The claim that religious authority is not in the members does not, then, interfere with the obvious responsibility that each and every member has for the efficacious service and genuine development of the religious congregation. Nor does it prevent the appropriate exercise of charisms of leadership on the part of many (maybe in some ways, on the part of *all*) members. But it does invite us to investigate the kind of authority that can be in all the members and the possible role that all the members play through their vow of obedience in mediating with the Church the religious authority that a superior always receives from God in Christ Jesus.

4) Is a superior necessary in every local community? In the last twenty years there has been a lot of experimentation and development in most congregations on this issue. This practice of having a superior in each local community has been stronger in the tradition of some institutes than in others. A number of local communities that experimented with not having a local superior have rediscovered the need and now have a superior again. Other communities involved in the same experiment continue without a local superior and do not see the need for one. Indeed I wonder whether some congregations have so moved away from local superiors that they would now consider this issue otiose.

There are some questions here for further genuine development. What have over fifteen years of experimentation taught us on this point? Could the answer to this question vary according to the tradition and charism of the religious institute? Can there be many other elements of a concrete local community that could determine the answer one way or the other? Or is it necessary for religious authority that there be a superior in every local community, or at least for a relatively contained area comprising several local communities?

5) What is the full meaning of the religious vow of obedience? The Vatican document on religious life is provoking some discussion on this question. In one section of the document we read: "The religious is pledged to obey the directives of lawful superiors according to the constitutions of the institute and further accepts a particular obedience to the Holy Father in virtue of the vow of obedience."[21] And in another section: "All religious are obliged to obey the Holy Father as their highest superior in virtue of the vow of obedience (canon 590, #2)."[22] Of course, simply as members of the Church there is expected an obedience, a support and a unity on the part of religious in relationship to the Holy Father. (For some members of the Society of Jesus there is a special obedience pledged to the Holy Father in virtue of the

Jesuit fourth vow to accept missions.)[23] However, the question here is about the vow that only religious take and that all religious take. What is this "particular obedience" to the Holy Father in virtue of the religious vow of obedience? Is something new being said here beyond any past understanding of the relationship in obedience of religious to the Holy Father?

I would hope that this present time of evaluation can provide an opportunity for us patiently to discuss some of these issues of confusion and conflict and to make some careful and decisive choices, so that with God's blessing a fruitful future development can bring a greater unity among us for corporate support and service in furthering the Reign of God's love in human hearts in the face of the great challenges of our world.

c) Religious Poverty.

In the third chapter of this book[24] I reflected on the trend of a distress over poverty in religious life. This trend continues with us and poses some further concerns at this juncture of special review and reflection. The economics of running a religious congregation is as difficult and trying as the running of many business corporations and the raising of a family today. Since money does not miraculously fall from the sky, the salaries that religious earn become very important. There must be mature responsibility for contributing to the community's needs and there must be none of that adolescent self-centeredness which can lead to living unnecessarily off the labor of others. Having said that, however, we must be extremely careful not to have, or seem to have, any policy that all religious must earn their own support. This could easily tip the balance of discernment of appropriate ministries in favor of works that have sufficient salaries attached—and away from services which, while not financially remunerative, are of great influence in furthering God's Kingdom of love and peace in human hearts.

The issue here is a carefully nuanced one and will be lost in a carelessly unrealistic over-simplification. At bottom, we are speaking here of an attitude in grace. It is an attitude of not owning "my" salary, or any other type of income either. When any income is seen as a gift acquired for all of us, both a sense of the corporate and a fundamental reliance on God's love and care can be deepened. In this way religious poverty can promote and keep alive religious community. And God, in and through the community, will be able to care for the needs of all, those whose work is salaried and those whose work is not. This religious poverty, most profoundly, becomes a community's relationship to material goods beyond any need for prestige, motivated by an attitude of total reliance on God's love and care. It becomes the graced freedom to make careful decisions solely for the greater service of that love in our world today. Then religious poverty, instead of being simply an individual matter, will have a more genuine, communal public witness and, finally, will stir insight and energy for greater ministerial service.

d) Apostolic Works.

The Vatican document also calls religious to reflect on the complicated area of apostolic works appropriate for each religious institute. Since Vatican II there has been much adaptation of apostolic works, and this has led to great diversification of ministries within religious life and within the whole Church.[25] And there has been a great multiplication of new, often individual ministries.

This would seem a good time to evaluate developments in this area. A clearly perceived sense of the corporate dimension of mission seems central to the nature of a religious institute. A group with a genuine corporate sense is meant to be something quite different from a loosely bound group of people working hard at their own jobs. The Vatican document speaks of "the mission itself undertaken as a community responsibility" and of "the integrity of the common apostolate (as) a particular responsibility of major superiors."[26] Some questions can perhaps facilitate reflection. Has the great diversification of ministries weakened our sense of corporate mission together? Have we weakened our corporate commitment to works traditional to our institute by fitting new ministries too much to the gifts, development and desires of individual members? Over these recent years, has there been not only a lessening of numbers involved in institutional education but also a loss of heart in our commitment to traditional works of education—primary, secondary and college/university? Is it time to regroup and with a whole new vision and appreciation of how central education is to human and Gospel development for all of us, courageously to recommit ourselves to an adapted, contemporary involvement in private and parochial education? Is it time, in reference to education as an apostolic instrument, to reassess what is the greater good, the more widespread good, the longer term good, the good more likely, finally, to influence structures, as we religious seek to serve faith, promote justice and align with the poor?

But in all of this, again, the point is subtle, not mechanical or one-dimensional. We are asking about an attitude of corporate service in light of the spirit of our congregation's founding experience. It is not a matter of all doing the same work. And it certainly is not a matter of ceasing all our new works and returning to the way things used to be.

e) Vocations to Religious Life.

In his letter to the American bishops, John Paul II spoke of the decline in numbers of religious as "a matter of grave concern to me" and he asked the commission he was appointing "to analyze the reasons for this decline in vocations . . . with a view to encouraging a new growth and a fresh move forward in this most important sector of the Church's life."[27] In Chapter Four[28] I mentioned our need to broaden our understanding of vocation beyond that of the religious and priestly. The need for and the actual development of vibrant, generous lay vocations continues to characterize contemporary American spirituality. And this development must not be ended nor be seen as an interference to the growth of priestly and religious vocations.

Nonetheless, we are left in a quandary. Nor is there yet light enough clearly to see our way. The growing secularization of our world has effected a whole sea-change in the way a religious vocation is viewed now, in contrast to thirty years ago. For women, when religious life and priesthood are seen as states of life involving serious oppression and

163

discrimination, the view can become still more negative. And because of some serious doubts about the possibility and nature of a life-commitment —something quite different from a career—young people are waiting longer and longer to choose their way of life. Among generous, dedicated young people in college or after, how do we help those for whom it is right to recognize and take the risk of following a religious vocation? Having realized in a way we often did not in the past that many generous gifted graduates are meant to develop serious lay vocations, the question remains: How are we to help those among them who are called to religious life to recognize and actuate that potential for profound faith and that intimate sense of God's love that can reveal such a call?

I have felt this quandry often in my own university work over the past few years. There is a whole set of natural fears in many young people that prevents serious consideration of a religious vocation. What will other students think of them? Can they be happy in a permanent celibate life-style? Is God and God's love real enough to sustain their enthusiasm and energy over the years in a celibate life-style? Do they want to be publicly committed to the Church in such a special way? Is religious life an apt way of dealing with many of the world's critical problems? How attractive do they find the actual lived witness and life-style of religious they know?

My comments here are surely no answer to the question of decline in religious vocations. They only mean to articulate some aspects of this difficult problem. It is a problem that we must seriously and carefully analyze, with great patience and trust in the Lord of the harvest who asks that we pray for the sending of laborers into the harvest. But we must also learn how to recognize and encourage people who are being called to that intimate dedication to the absoluteness of God's love in Jesus in the public consecration called religious life.[29]

4. Forgiveness and Reconciliation: A Catechesis of the Human Heart. The October meeting of the sixth international synod of bishops was devoted to "Reconciliation and Penance in the Mission of the Church." It provoked, in many articles preliminary to its meeting, a renewed awareness of the problems connected with the Sacrament of Reconciliation in the Church. My 1980 and 1983 reflections, now Chapters One and Four of this book, both recognized the situation among us of confusion and timidity regarding acknowledgment of personal sin and the effect this has on our exercise of ministry. And I made the suggestion that what was needed was "a whole catechesis to help people recognize in their own hearts the dynamic of receiving God's gift of forgiveness."[30] It is this final point that I would like to develop further in light of the evaluation being done of the Sacrament of Penance and Reconciliation.

The confusion previously referred to touches on an essential aspect of Christian experience and identity in our world. The Christian lives a *process* of being saved rather than a *state* of salvation. In Jesus God's loving redemption of every person has been revealed, promised and accomplished. But the Christian life is a matter of assimilating daily in our own heart and consciousness this victory of God's loving forgiveness in

165

Jesus. This daily assimilation and transformation is not always explicitly conscious. But neither is it automatic and pre-determined. Though it is all the work of a loving God, real cooperation of weak, free human persons is always needed.

An essential aspect of this central process of transformation is a healthy, salvific sense of one's sinfulness. Many people are still trying to shed past un-salvific experiences of their sinfulness. And this leaves them with a confusion, a timidity and, at times, even a denial of sin. But our salvation by God, which is always a matter of our forgiveness in Jesus, requires that we learn to recognize and cooperate with the dynamic involved in a salvific sense of our sinfulness. The confusion and timidity must be dispelled. And slowly, in some circles, this is happening. Many religious in the past few years have shared with me their own profound experience of their sinfulness leading to a much deeper, more faithful, more enthusiastic joy in God's loving, gratuitous forgiveness revealed in Jesus' Calvary experience.[31]

Nothing can replace this interior experience of being saved and forgiven in our own sinfulness. Without much of a salvific sense of sinfulness, there cannot be much of a profound experience of God's saving forgiveness. And this must affect those results that always accompany an experience of God's forgiveness: a deep joy in the intimacy of God's love and an enthusiastic desire for ministry with and in Jesus. The character of our apostolic action, then, responds directly to the quality of our experience as forgiven sinners.

The issue does not concern God's forgiveness in itself. It is a matter of the dynamic of faith in human experience whereby God's transforming forgiveness is received into a human heart and consciousness. What is needed is a catechesis of the human heart whereby individuals can recognize and cooperate with the inner journey of forgiveness that is somehow happening within every human person.

Renewed rites of the Sacraments of Reconciliation and of Eucharist cannot replace this catechesis of heart. Both of these renewed rites are real blessings. But there is something they do not necessarily accomplish. The renewed rite of reconciliation in 1974 obviously has not resolved the problem with that sacrament. The executive director of a diocesan liturgical commission claimed over a year ago: "At the rate things are going, the sacrament will cease to exist in ten years because of nonuse. At least two generations now have made no use of it at all. . . . The reform so far has failed miserably."[32] Others would claim that the decline in use of the Sacrament of Penance and Reconciliation is due to the splendid renewal of the Eucharistic liturgy. In an article in *America* Ed Marciniak, as he reflects on the amazing effects of the renewed Eucharistic liturgy whereby the faithful now "immerse themselves in the celebration—with heart, mind and body," claims that "they can now enjoy the acts and words of forgiveness."[33] There is some truth to this, and it is something for which to be grateful to God. But those "acts and words of forgiveness" can be quite superficial—without implying blame for the people themselves—unless they are accompanied by some important interior dispositions and realizations. Without an honest admission of personal sin, without a clarity in faith about the disappointment our sin represents before a forgiving God, and without much of an experience of embarrassment, shame and genuine sorrow before a God whose love never falters, the transforming effect of God's forgiveness in us is almost certain to be slight and shallow—and therefore incapable of the decisiveness that leads to genuine conversion. The human heart must be catechised to the signs and to the usually measured pace of the inner journey of God's forgiveness. I strongly incline to the view that something more is needed for that than even a vital, renewed Eucharistic liturgy.

In the wake of the synod on reconciliation and penance there are serious issues to be analyzed as we try to evaluate our present posture and steer a decisive course for future growth. Without a clearer and more decisively salvific sense of our sinfulness—that basic tendency not to take God seriously that can well up, even unconsciously, in all our hearts—without a better sense of that sinfulness, our experience of forgiveness and reconciliation will be muddled and mild, whether that experience is occasioned by the Eucharist, by a communal penance service or by the individual use of the Sacrament of Reconciliation. We need to find ways so that human hearts can be catechised to profound experiences of God's forgiveness with the help of parents, moral theologians, religious educators, spiritual directors, homilists, friends and many other people in various situations.

5. Eucharist and Community. The renewed Eucharistic liturgy, just mentioned above, has brought a greater sense of community to the Church and her celebrations. The Eucharist is not simply a "me and Jesus" experience but rather a gathering of brothers and sisters in the Lord to share their faith and celebrate God's love in their midst. And yet undoubtedly in many situations, perhaps especially in certain parishes, the appreciation of this communal dimension of the Eucharist requires much greater development.

But the increased sensitivity to the community dimension of the Eucharist is also raising some confusion and tensions among us. Rather frequently at inter-denominational workshops or meetings, non-Catholics feel the tension of the question as to whether they should receive communion at a Catholic Eucharist. And while theological dialogues among denominations sometimes publicly are suggesting that there is enough shared understanding of the Eucharist for regular inter-communion, the official Church position restricts inter-communion. And this divergence causes confusion among the faithful. There is no question that great pain can be involved for Catholics and non-Catholics in not communicating together where deeply shared experiences also seem to invite expression in a shared Eucharist. But at least in some cases, such experience of pain may be very appropriate, allowing, as it does, the Eucharist, the sacrament of unity, to point up the lack of unity which oftentimes is only confusedly experienced and acknowledged. Furthermore, to resolve all tension by making the Eucharist universally available to anybody anywhere would seem gravely to betray the depth of Catholic faith and doctrine that is meant to be shared and celebrated in that experience. Though there is a greater tendency in groups now to inter-communion, some of this confusion and tension will remain, and it will require the combined reflection of sacramental theologians, pastoral ministers and others of the faithful.

Concelebration continues to be basically a great blessing in the Church. But certainly operationally, and maybe theoretically too, certain questions and confusions seem to have risen over the past few years. What difference does vesting make? In more and more groups, while the presiding priest vests, other priests vest less and less—and, at times, feel less and less free to vest. Vesting, at this point in our history, seems to many to segregate some members from the community rather than to symbolize one of a number of special roles played in the one Eucharistic community. And it is often seen to heighten the women's concern about a solely male priesthood. Indeed, quite aside from the question of vesting, growing numbers of persons, both women and men—including priests and liturgists—are clearly, by both word and behavior, seeking to discourage concelebration itself. It is not my concern here to resolve these tensions, but simply to articulate their occurrence in the Christian community at this point, with the hope that we can patiently live with them, carefully assess them and come to whatever resolutions in the future can make us more one in both life and Eucharist.

One final point here: It is happening with increasing frequency now that in workshops or meetings in which some aspects of the Christian mystery have been reflected on, the Eucharist is quite consciously not included as part of the whole experience. It may be that some of the confusions and tensions mentioned above explain this omission on the part of certain priests and of others planning such meetings. However, I personally wonder if it is not misleading, and even dangerously impoverishing in the long run, for a Christian and Catholic community to gather for a day or longer, precisely as a religious gathering, and to omit the Eucharist, the sacrament of thanksgiving and obedience to God, as part of its celebration.

6. A Spirituality of Justice and Liberation. It is impossible to survey trends and issues in American spirituality and not mention once again our continuing struggle to develop an integrated spirituality of justice and liberation. I have reviewed this area in two earlier chapters,[34] but some further developments may deserve comment. John Paul's courageous visits to Central America and to Poland have kept the ministry of the promotion of Christian justice very much in the limelight. And his continuing prophetic calls for peace, justice and unity through dialogue and diplomacy are striking evidence of spirituality in action.

But despite hard work by various groups and a growing development toward a more integrated spirituality, a certain, rather quiet polarization continues between concerns of justice and those of faith and spirituality. There is a growing group of believers who are becoming more informed about the social and international complexity of systematic justice issues, but not always as related to a genuine and lively experience of prayer and the religious dimension. At the other end of the spectrum are those whose sense of religion and practice of prayer and regular and genuine, but who are not that explicitly involved with issues of public injustice. Of course this is no hard and fast division. It is rather a tendency strongly among us, and most of us would fit under one tendency or the other. And neither of the two is to be completely condemned, much less accused of heresy—as sometimes at least equivalently occurs.

But both groups need to move steadily—it is a journey—to a more integrating service of faith and justice. Dialogue, and the continuing, honest acknowledgment of the partial inadequacy of each one's present situation, is needed to aid a greater unity in an integrated spirituality. Each of the polarities in question presents a different challenge, must therefore be dealt with differently, and each requires different experiences for the growth that is needed. Those whose center of gravity is more with prayer and with the explicitly religious need to be stretched by the challenge of appropriate experiences of social service situations, whereas those whose gravity centers chiefly in the daily struggles for liberation of people from unjust situations and/or in the technicalities of social analysis need to root their energies, studies and work in a prayerful faith and a directly religious motivation. The different needs of these two groups could be taken into account in determining retreat experiences and special sabbatical programs.

The profoundly Trinitarian nature of the Christian life must be the genuine motivation for any ministry for justice. Without wanting to be judgmental, one does not always sense this profoundly religious motivation. On the other hand, one does not always see a Trinitarian experience explode into energy for justice concerns. At times, it can seem as though interest in and concern about Jesus' experience of his Father is a wasteful luxury or an unrealistic sentimentality. Rather, it is precisely there in our contemplative experience of Jesus' passionate desire for his Father and his Father's faithful blessing of love on his Son that we find forged an energy and hope and enthusiasm that can motivate all our ventures and can withstand all trials and dangers of injustice. Our serious social analysis (terribly necessary in itself) and work for justice must be contextualized in a decisive faith perspective and a carefully religious sensitivity.

7. *The Bishops' Pastoral on Peace and War.* My comments on this topic in the previous chapter and the promulgation of the final approved text of the bishops' pastoral spur further, brief reflections here. Obviously, widespread, intense, if by no means universal, study and education have followed the approval of almost a year ago. Programs, workshops, courses, articles are available very nearly everywhere. Actually, reaction to the final, as compared with the second, draft seems muted. Various reasons for the relatively quiet reception suggest themselves. The document is so long that perhaps not many have read it carefully. Maybe some are guessing (hoping?) that this pastoral, like so many others, will not be given much serious attention in the long run. Further, whether they have read the final version or not, some give much credence to the report that the bishops toned down (backed down from?) an earlier strong stand represented in the second draft—and therefore, so the view goes, the promulgated version really doesn't say much and can be ignored. Others, in-

cluding the government, know very well that the letter
says a great deal and, once their efforts failed to prevent episcopal approval of the final draft's measured
but still strong and challenging witness, many who
opposed the bishops for speaking at all or for speaking as they did have chosen a strategy either of complete silence or of a few pleasant words suggesting
that the letter is amateurish, or bland. And for those
who not only believe in personally but also insist upon
prescribing for everyone nothing less than an absolute
pacifist stance, the letter is, of course, seen as a
failure of moral and political courage and, according-
ly, as worth little attention.

But quiet agreement with the bishops has also
grown, over the last year especially, among many,
many Catholics and other Americans—as a more extensive awareness continues to develop about the
serious dangers which the stockpiling of nuclear
weapons all over the world poses to our human
future. For Catholics particularly, the letter itself is,
furthermore, an ecclesiological education on at least
two counts. And the long-term results of that education may be monumental in areas far beyond the
crucial one of peace and nuclear armaments. First,
there is the process of the letter: a three year public
dialogue, among the bishops themselves (with the
disagreements between them there for all who watch
T.V. to see), between the bishops and the Holy See
and other episcopal conferences, between the bishops
and the government, between the bishops and
theologians, military experts, economists, and so
forth—and, very importantly, between the bishops
and the faithful. Second, the completed letter
forcefully projected clear distinctions by the bishops

themselves among universally binding moral statements in the letter; strongly held convictions of the majority of the bishops, from which, however, other bishops and any lay person, following careful reflection, are free to dissent; and simply prudential applications of moral principles or insights to concrete situations or views, judgments about which are wide open to legitimate dispute.

The pastoral also contributed greatly to the community of believers everywhere in asserting—and against much opposition and criticism—that morality is public as well as private, societal as well as personal, that public and political issues are frequently also moral issues and that, insofar as they are so, there is not only the right but there is the obligation for all religious people to be concerned and, especially for religious leaders, to become suitably informed—and then to speak.

8. Christian Revelation and the Human Sciences. Here I want simply to point to something, the discussion of which lies far beyond the ken of a survey such as this, but something which, for all its sophistication and difficulty, nevertheless works very directly on all spiritual life—both the spiritual life of persons and the spiritual life of groups. I am speaking chiefly of the social sciences, like psychology, sociology, anthropology and economics, but my concern can also, at times, involve the hard sciences like biology and physics.

In thinking of these sciences I am viewing them both in themselves and as they relate to Christian revelation. My point is twofold. First, these disciplines usually carry within them, often as a matter of necessity if the discipline is to exist at all, a series of assumptions and presuppositions, which, precisely as assumed and presupposed, are not demonstrated according to the methods of verification proper to that discipline. Therefore though powerfully operative, these assumptions are usually *silently* operative, since the discipline assumes them rather than deals with them. Sometimes this quietly smuggled element in a given science is a matter explicitly recognized by those working in that science. In other cases, the person seriously involved in the science, but without a background in philosophy, may be largely or wholly unaware of the often silent, but immense influence at work in the very foundation of the science in question.

These assumptions and presuppositions powerfully affect the conclusions these disciplines come to on very concrete issues, including issues very intimately related to value questions and religious questions. Where these assumptions or presuppositions are hostile to spiritual life or are seriously deficient in their views of spiritual life, then the influence of psychology, sociology and many other sciences must be of the greatest interest to those concerned with spirituality. (I am obviously leaving entirely aside here the enormous actual good, the enormous potential for good, these sciences represent for spirituality.)

My second point may be briefer. When science becomes scientism, then any discipline, whether only operatively or also theoretically, becomes a norm ultimate to Christian revelation and the life of faith. Then the discipline sits in judgment on revelation and decides what revelation may and may not say or mean, and what the life of faith may and may not be. In such a situation, most urgent questions arise both for theology and for the philosophy of religion. And these questions will always have direct, practical effects both on spirituality and on spiritual life itself. This problem of course is not new. And it continues to show its destructive effects, sometimes strongly, in connection with this and other related issues, within the community of believers. It is important for us to notice this.[35]

Conclusion

The tasks of spiritual life, whether personal or corporate, do not, in any final way, ever reach term. Obviously not, because we are talking about life. And so the growth, the change, the experimentation, must continue. But as was seen at least as long ago as Socrates, life well lived is examined, it is reflected on, making new choices possible, necessary, inevitable—even the choice, at times, to confirm a previous decision and direction. All this is conventional wisdom. But in the lives of busy apostolic persons and busy apostolic groups, it is likely wisdom too much honored from afar. And so, in my judgment, it may need saying anew just now, and it certainly needs to be followed through on, even as our spiritual journey continues—hopefully a still vigorous, creative, adventurous journey, but one presently taking place in a special moment calling for careful assessment and choice. May the assessing and the choosing deepen the journey and its high purpose: the praise and service of our dear God throughout the world. The psalmist says it—at once a statement and a summons to us all: "How great is your name, O Lord our God, through all the earth."[36]

CONCLUSION

Somehow it seems appropriate that this book end right in the midst of things and so have a certain incompleteness about it. Spiritual trends will continue to form, to develop, to clarify, to challenge and to carry us into the future. The rich, bustling journey of life continues. I hope that this book has served not only to sensitize readers to some developments and directions of American spirituality, but also to stimulate them to adapt and complete their own stocktaking and reflection. In a rapidly shifting, changing world and in a Church whose future we are called upon to choose in the Spirit, it becomes more and more important for informed believers to have a sense of contemporary spiritual trends and issues.

We all have a role to play in this choice of our future in the Spirit. It is exciting. And it requires real wisdom and courage. It will not always be easy. To recognize and to choose, again and again, precisely within these shifting, changing trends of our time, the one perennial truth and beauty of God's revelation in Jesus is the difficult and challenging task facing us as believers. The Letter to the Hebrews speaks to the steadfast center of the enterprise: "Christ yesterday, today and the same forever."[1] And Hopkins catches splendidly the variety and difference of that journey, common to us all, our journey into God: "Christ plays in ten thousand places, lovely in limbs and lovely in eyes not His, to the Father, through the features of men's faces."[2]

Though this book has touched on many specific trends, topics and issues, it has centrally been about God—a God whose Spirit we seek in all the trends of our day and whose Spirit beckons us into the future; a God whose love, at times, can mesmerize our hearts in quiet contemplation and, at other times, can fire our hearts for staunch service; but always a God whose mystery and intimacy invites us beyond our wildest imaginings.

Much evidence seems to suggest that we will be led more and more to the Calvary of an apparently dark, empty stillness, perhaps appalled at the latest display of inhuman violence. And there we must learn to find a God of love and fidelity beyond any power of evil in this world—a God of quiet joy and dogged hope patiently revealed in the eloquent beauty of a Son's faithful obedience in the dark and empty stillness. And that fidelity and obedience is always blessed with Resurrection. It always gives light. We must learn to recognize our God on the dark journey.

NOTES

Chapter One

[1]For another format and a more extensive treatment of individual thematic trends in spirituality, consult the series of articles by Matthew Fox, O.P. and others in *Spirituality Today* beginning in the Mar, 1978 issue.

[2]Cf. Karl Rahner, S.J., *Theological Investigations, vol 3, The Theology of the Spiritual Life,* tr. Karl-H and Boniface Kruger, "The Ignatian Mysticism of Joy in the World" (Baltimore: Helicon, 1967), pp. 277-293. What Rahner describes as the *fuga saeculi* for a Jesuit is fundamental to any mature Christian life with and in God.

[3]*Rom* 7/14-25.

[4]Cf. my article, "Forgiveness," *Sisters Today,* Dec, 1973, pp. 185-192.

[5]Cf. John R. Donahue, S,J,, "Biblical Perspectives on Justice" in *The Faith That Does Justice,* ed. John C. Haughey, S.J. (New York: Paulist, 1977), pp. 68-112 and José Porfirio Miranda, *Marx and the Bible,* tr. John Eagleson (Maryknoll, NY: Orbis, 1974), 338 pp.

[6]Jürgen Moltmann, *The Crucified God* (New York: Harper & Row, 1974), 346 pp., Jon Sobrino, S.J., *Christology At the Crossroads,* tr. John Drury (Maryknoll, NY: Orbis, 1978), 432 pp., Leonardo Boff, *Jesus Christ Liberator* (Maryknoll, NY: Orbis, 1978).

[7]Cf. Richard A. Blake, S.J., " 'As the Father Has Sent Me' ", *America,* Aug 25, 1979, pp. 66-69 and William J. Byron, S.J., "Privatization—A Contemporary Challenge to Ignatian Spirituality," *Chicago Studies,* vol. 14, No. 3, Fall, 1975, pp. 241-251.

[8]Elisabeth Kübler-Ross, *On Death and Dying* (New York: Macmillan, 1969), 260 pp.

[9]Alvin Toffler, *Future Shock* (New York: Bantam, 1970), 561 pp.

[10]Cf. Matthew Fox, O.P., "Hermeneutic and Hagiography," *Spirituality Today,* Sept, 1978, p. 263.

[11]Cf. Leonard Doohan, "The Spiritual Value of Leisure," *Spirituality Today,* June, 1979, pp. 157-167.

[12]*Gal* 5/16-26.

[13]Cf. John C. Haughey, S.J., "Jesus '79 and Christian Unity," *America,* Mar 31, 1979, pp. 250-253 and Kevin Ranaghan, "Jesus '79: Another View" with Fr. Haughey's response in *America,* May 19, 1979, pp. 409-412. Also Fr. Haughey's talk in the Proceedings of the Chicago Conference, *Theological Reflections on the Charismatic Renewal* (Ann Arbor: Servant Books, 1978), pp. 99-124.

[14]Other terms can be used to designate the person in whom religious authority resides in some special way. My use of the term "superior" does not imply that this is the only term, nor the most suitable in some instances. The key thing is that religious authority is recognized by all to reside in this person.

[15]I developed this further in an article which appeared in *The Way Supplement*, Spring, 1980.

[16]Johannes B. Metz, *Followers of Christ* (New York: Paulist, 1978), p. 42f.

[17]On a completely different topic, but one not unrelated to affectivity and sexuality, there is the question of the sexual language by which we refer to God, whether as Father or as Mother, etc. This is not an unimportant topic, but I do not treat it in this article.

[18]Metz, *op cit,* p. 48ff.

[19]Cf. James Walsh, S.J., "The Poverty of the Gospel Community," *The Way Supplement,* No. 34, Autumn, 1978, pp. 107-116.

[20]Cf. Henri J.M. Nouwen, *Clowning in Rome* (New York: Image, 1979), Chapter 1.

[21]Metz, *op cit,* p. 12.

[22]*Ibid.,* p. 18-22.

[23]Cf article on this document in *Review for Religious,* Jan, 1979, pp. 21-27.

Chapter Two

[1]Cf. William J. Byron, S.J., "Liberal Learning and the Future of Families," *America,* June 14, 1980, pp. 499-502.

[2]Cf. Bishop J. Francis Stafford, "An Agenda for a National Family Policy," *America,* June 14, 1980, pp. 495-498.

[3]Cf. Stanley Hauerwas, "The Moral Meaning of the Family," *Commonweal,* Aug 1, 1980, pp. 432-436.

[4]Paul C. Vitz, *Psychology as Religion* (Grand Rapids: Wm. B. Erdmans Publishing Co., 1977), p. 9.

[5]Though Vitz's book may not acknowledge enough some of the valuable contributions of Fromm, Rodgers, Maslow and May, his critique of the damage done by those popularizers of selfist psychology who propose it almost as a substitute national religion seems accurate and incisive. He is quick to acknowledge that such popularizers "have pushed the ideas of these four theorists to extremes for which they should not be held responsible" (p. 28).

[6]*Ibid.*, p. 105.

[7]*Ibid.*, p. 135.

[8]*Lk* 9/23-25.

[9]Vitz, *op. cit.*, p. 107.

[10]Cf. supra, p. 7f

[11]In a talk given on Oct, 11, 1966.

[12]Cf. my article, "Prayer, Mission and Obedience," *The Way Supplement*, No. 37, Spring, 1980, pp. 50-57 where I spelled out in more detail how authority can be a special servant of apostolic unity.

[13]Cf. "A Report on Parish Renewal" by Bishop Edward O'Leary, Chairperson of US Bishops Ad Hoc Committee on the Parish in *Origins,* N.C. Documentary Service, Nov 20, 1980, pp. 367-368 to see the bishops' awareness of the need to develop the parish ministry.

[14]Cf. my article, "Hidden in Jesus before the Father," *Review for Religious,* Jan 1975, pp. 129-130.

[15]Cf. supra, p. 34 on the freedom to die. The phrase is from Johannes B. Metz, *Followers of Christ* (New York: Paulist, 1978), pp. 18-22.

[16]Cf. *The Way Supplement*, No. 36, Summer, 1979 and No. 37, Spring, 1980 for help on this issue.

[17]Cf. "A Symposium on the Place of Daily Mass in the Life of a Jesuit," *Worship,* vol. 44, No. 5, pp. 277-291.

[18]It will be important not to exaggerate John Paul's apparent conservatism as Mary Durkin suggests in *America,* "The Pope, Genesis and Human Sexuality," Sept 27,

1980, pp. 166-170 when she concludes a study of the Pope's developing reflections on the Book of Genesis with the claim: "Pope John Paul, who appears to some as a conservative theologian, has developed a theology of the body and of sexuality that appears far from conservative; some would even consider it revolutionary."

[19]Cf. Robert F. Morneau, "Redemptor Hominis: Themes and Theses," *Review for Religious,* Mar, 1980, pp. 247-262 and Ronald Modras, "The Moral Philosophy of Pope John Paul II," *Theological Studies,* Dec, 1980, pp. 683-697.

[20]Cf. supra, p. 36f.

[21]Cf. Walter J. Burghardt, S.J., "Academe and Arena," *The Catholic Mind*, June, 1980, p. 21.

[22]Archbishop John Quinn's report on the Synod at the US bishops' meeting in Washington, DC on Nov 10-13, 1980, "Collegiality and Faith," *Origins,* N.C. Documentary Service, Nov 20, 1980, p. 355.

[23]Cf. "To Speak the Truth in Love," unpublished version of Sr. Theresa Kane's talk to the Leadership Conference of Women Religious in Phila. on Aug 24, 1980.

Chapter Three

[1]Cf. supra, p. 44ff.

[2]John A. Coleman, S.J., "The Situation for Modern Faith," *Theological Studies,* Dec, 1978, p. 604, where he is citing Huston Smith, "Secularization and the Sacred," in Donald Cutler, ed., *The Religious Situation 1969,* Boston, 1969, p. 583.

[3]Coleman, *loc. cit.,* citing Huston, *art. cit.,* p. 587.

[4]Coleman, *art. cit.,* p. 605, citing Guy E. Swanson, "Modern Secularity," in Cutler, *op. cit.,* pp. 803-804.

[5]Cf. supra, p. 45ff.

[6]To speak of God *above* the world is, of course, not to make a spatial delineation. Rather, it is to speak of a God whose being and love is far greater than this world. In Jn 12/32, Jesus' words remind us that ultimately we are attracted ("seduced" is the Old Testament word) to this experience of God. It is not simply our own, Pelagian choice.

[7]*Ps* 63/3.

[8]Cf. *1 Cor* 15/22-28.

[9]In *Origins,* Aug 13, 1981, "The Unmet Challenges of Vatican II," p. 148.

[10]Sequndo Galilea, "Liberation as an Encounter with Politics and Contemplation," in Claude Geffré and Gustavo Guttiérez, eds., *The Mystical and Political Dimension of the Christian Faith* (New York, 1974), p. 20.

[11]*Ibid.,* p. 28.

[12]Cf. supra, p. 49ff.

[13]Karl Rahner, S.J., "Towards a Fundamental Theological Interpretation of Vatican II" *Theological Studies,* Dec, 1979, (Leo J. O'Donovan, S.J., tr.), p. 717.

[14]Murnion, *Origins,* Aug 13, 1981, *loc. cit.*

[15]*Ibid.,* p. 147.

[16]Cf. *Jn* 17/22.

[17]Sandra M. Schneiders, I.H.M., "Theological Trends: Ministry and Ordination: I," *The Way,* Oct, 1980, p. 291.

[18]Cf. John A. Coleman, S.J., "The Future of Ministry," *America,* Mar 28, 1981, pp. 243-249.

[19]Schneiders, *art. cit.,* pp. 290-299.

[20]Cf. my article, "Prayer, Mission and Obedience," *The Way Supplement,* No. 37, Spring, 1980, pp. 50-57.

[21]*Ibid.,* p. 55.

[22]In the translation by Huub Oosterhuis et al, *Fifty Psalms* (New York: Herder and Herder, 1969), p. 74.

[23]Cf. supra, p. 48f

[24]In *Family Weekly Sunday Magazine* for March 22, 1981, p. 11.

[25]Cf. Bishop J. Francis Stafford's excellent article, "The Year of the Family Revisited," *America,* May 16, 1981, pp. 399-403.

[26]"Dialogue on Women in the Church: Interim Report," *Origins,* June 25, 1981, p. 81.

[27]Schneiders, "Theological Trends: Ministry and Ordination II: The Ordination of Women," *The Way,* April, 1981, p. 148.

[28]Mary F. Rousseau, "Theological Trends: The Ordination of Women: A Philosopher's Viewpoint," *The Way,* July, 1981, p. 224.

[29]*National Catholic Reporter,* July 17, 1981, p. 1.

[30]Cf. supra, p. 28.

[31]Murnion, *art. cit.,* p. 151.

[32]*Ibid.* Also Schneiders, *art. cit., The Way,* April, 1981, p. 142.

[33]Cf. supra, p. 36f and p. 66ff.

[34]Cf. Coleman, *art. cit., America,* Mar 28, 1981, pp. 247-248.

[35]For a challenging, optimistic view of seminary formation for the future, cf. Bishop Walter Sullivan's address, "What Priesthood Awaits the Semenarian?" *Origins,* Sept. 17, 1981, pp. 209-215.

Chapter Four

[1]Cf. supra, p. 73.

[2]Cf. supra, p. 81ff.

[3]*The Deeper Life,* Louis Dupré (New York: Crossroad, 1981).

[4]*Ibid.,* p. 46.

[5]*Mt* 6/18.

[6]*Karl Rahner, Theological Investigations XX, Concern for the Church,* tr. Edward Quinn (New York: Crossroad, 1981), p. 149.

[7]Avery Dulles, S.J. is always a helpful and carefully creative guide in this whole question of the Church. Cf. his *Models of the Church* (New York: Image, 1978) and his more recent book, *A Church to Believe In* (New York: Crossroad, 1982).

[8]Cf. supra, p. 49ff.

[9]Cf. supra, p. 13ff.

[10]"The Dimensions of Care," *Origins,* Jan 28, 1982, pp. 520-524.

[11]Tad Guzie, *The Book of Sacramental Basics* (New York: Paulist, 1981), p. 85.

[12]*Ibid.,* pp. 97-103.

[13]"The Future of Church and Ministry," *Origins,* May 6, 1982, p. 750.

[14]"What the Laity Need," *Origins,* May 20, 1982, pp. 9-15, esp. 14.

[15]Cf. supra, p. 102ff.

[16]*America,* Nov 13, 1982, p. 284. Since we are in the midst of a process with regard to the pastoral letter of the bishops on peace and war, it may be helpful to the reader to know that these remarks of mine were written in December, 1982.

[17]Cf. supra, p. 15ff.

[18]Johannes B. Metz, *Followers of Christ* (New York: Paulist, 1978) esp. pp. 41-44.

[19]*The Social Teaching of John Paul II,* No. 4: "The Theme of Liberation," presented by Rev. Roger Heckel, S.J., Pontifical Commission on Justice and Peace, Vatican City, 1980, esp. pp. 16-17. Heckel shows that John Paul II does not use the word liberation very much, and that when he does so, God and Christ are the subject and content of the liberation.

[20]Cf. supra, p. 85f.

[21]"The Changing Relations Between Bishops and Theologians," *Origins,* June 17, 1982, p. 70.

[22]Cf. supra, p. 8f.

[23]Cf. John C. Futrell, S.J., "The Monk and the Apostle," *Review for Religious,* May/June, 1982, p. 409.

[24]Thomas Merton, *The Monastic Journey,* ed. Br. Patrick Hart, (New York: Image, 1978), p. 213.

[25]Dupré, *op. cit.,* p. 43.

[26]Merton, *op. cit.,* pp. 213-217.

[27]Dupré, *op. cit.*

[28]Cf. supra, p. 95ff, and James T. Burtchaell, "The Future of Our Fellowship," *Commonweal,* June 18, 1982, pp. 364-368.

[29]Cf. Richard A. Hill, S.J., "The Community and the Option of Non-Canonical Status," *Review for Religious,* July/Aug, 1982, pp. 542-550. The author treats the issues involved in a congregation's moving to non-canonical status.

[30]Cf. supra, p. 97.

[31]Cf. supra, p. 88.

Chapter Five

[1]*Origins,* July 7, 1983, pp. 133-142.

[2]"Archbishop Quinn Discusses the Commission on Religious Life," *Origins,* July 7, 1983, p. 145.

[3]Cf. supra, p. 88ff.

[4]Cf. supra, p. 126ff, where I comment a bit on this issue.

[5]Some people might label the stage I am describing here as adolescent. And we usually put a pejorative meaning on

this term. I do not intend this pejorative meaning and I do not think it is necessary. I prefer to see this as a necessary developmental stage involved in all new growth—growth which may take place at any age. And, in the examples I have given, it is a stage of growth toward something very valuable and well worth the costs involved.

[6]*Origins,* July 7, 1983, p. 134, #10.

[7]*Ibid.,* p. 138, #34.

[8]Cf. supra, p. 95ff.

[9]*Origins,* July 7, 1983, p. 138, #34.

[10]*Ibid.,* p. 142, #37.

[11]For example, *cf.* the memorandum and report to the members of the Leadership Conference of Women Religious, 6 June 1983, from Sr. Helen Flaherty, SC, reporting on a meeting of four LCWR representatives with members of the Sacred Congregation for Religious and Secular Institutes in Rome on 9 May 1983.

[12]Cf. Avery Dulles, S.J., "The Teaching Authority of Bishops' Conferences," *America,* June 11, 1983, pp. 453-455.

[13]September/October 1982, volume 226.

[14]*Origins,* July 7, 1983, p. 140, #49.

[15]*Ibid.,* #50.

[16]Cf. Nadine Foley, O.P., "The Leadership of Women Religious: An Expendable Resource," *New Catholic World,* September/October 1982, p. 228. The full sentence at issue here is: "For American women religious, schooled in an ideology of democratic, self-initiating behaviour,

upon whom the highly regimented practices of traditional religious observance had ceased to rest lightly, it meant claiming authority over their own lives while sustaining their basic commitment to the enduring values of religious life and to the mission of the Gospel." I do not mean to imply that this approach is necessarily incompatible with the exercise of religious authority by a superior. But it would take some further discussion to integrate the two approaches.

[17]Cf. Mary Linscott, SND., "The Service of Religious Authority: Reflections on Government in the Revision of Constitutions," *Review for Religious,* Mar/Apr 1983, p. 212.

[18]*Ibid.,* p. 198.

[19]*Ibid.,* p. 210.

[20]*Origins,* ly 7, 1983, p. 140, #49.

[21]*Ibid.,* p. 135, #16.

[22]*Ibid.,* p. 141, #24.

[23]Cf. John W. O'Malley, S.J., "The Fourth Vow in Its Ignatian Context—A Historical Study," *Studies in the Spirituality of Jesuits,* Jan, 1983.

[24]Cf. supra, p. 100ff.

[25]*Ibid.,* p. 196.

[26]*Origins,* July 7, 1983, p. 136, #25.

[27]*Ibid.,* p. 132-133.

[28]Cf. supra, p. 123ff.

[29]*Origins,* July 7, 1983, p. 134, #5-12, esp. #10.

[30]Cf. supra, p. 121 and see also, for a related discussion, supra, p. 13ff.

[31]Sometimes these experiences are shared with me because they were initiated by my article, "Forgiveness," *Sisters Today,* Dec, 1973.

[32]James Breig, "What *U.S. Catholic* Readers Think About Confession," *U.S. Catholic,* Oct, 1982, p. 13.

[33]"The Sacrament of Penance: A Report From the Pews," *America,* July 16, 1983, p. 27.

[34]Cf. supra, p. 15ff. and p. 126ff.

[35]I have personally found helpful, in connection with this and other related issues, an effort to listen carefully to some of the central points in Ralph Martin's *A Crisis of Truth,* (Ann Arbor: Servant, 1982), 250 pp.

[36]*Ps.* 8/1.

Conclusion

[1]*Heb.* 13/8.

[2]From the sonnet, "As kingfishers catch fire, dragonflies draw flame."